A SHORT HISTORY OF TRACTORS IN UKRAINIAN

Tanika Gupta

A SHORT HISTORY OF TRACTORS IN UKRAINIAN

adapted from the novel by Marina Lewycka

OBERON BOOKS
LONDON

WWW.OBERONBOOKS.COM

This adaptation first published in 2017 by Oberon Books Ltd
521 Caledonian Road, London N7 9RH
Tel: +44 (0) 20 7607 3637 / Fax: +44 (0) 20 7607 3629
e-mail: info@oberonbooks.com
www.bloomsbury.com

A catalogue record for this book is available from the British
Library.

PB ISBN: 9781786823366
E ISBN: 9781786823373

Visit www.bloomsbury.com to read more about all our books and to buy
them. You will also find features, author interviews and news of any
author events, and you can sign up for e-newsletters so that you're always
first to hear about our new releases.

A Short History of Tractors in Ukrainian was co-produced by Hull Truck Theatre and Hull UK City of Culture 2017. It was first performed at Hull Truck Theatre on 22 September 2017 with the following cast:

Geoffrey Beevers	NIKOLAI
Jack Fielding	STANISLAV
Polly Frame	LUDMILLA
Ruth Lass	NADEZDHA
Ana Marija Spasjovic	VALENTINA
Richard Standing	DUBOV
Philip Stewart	MIKE
Hilary Tones	VERA

CREATIVES

Based on the novel by	Marina Lewycka
Adaptor	Tanika Gupta
Director	Mark Babych
Set and Costume Designer	Patrick Connellan
Lighting Designer	Paul Keogan
Composer	Sophie Cotton
Sound Designer	Ed Clarke
Voice/Dialect Coach	Natalie Grady
Movement Director	Deborah Pugh
Fight Director	Renny Krupinski
Assistant Director	Amanda Huxtable
Dramaturg	Ola Animashawun

CASTING

Lucy Jenkins CDG
Sookie McShane CDG

PRODUCTION

Producer	Elizabeth Jones
Head of Production & Technical	Amy Clarey
Production Manager	Luke Child

SET BUILDERS
Harrogate Theatre Scenic Services

STAGE MANAGEMENT

Company Stage Manager	Edward Salt
Deputy Stage Manager	Jane Williamson
Assistant Stage Manager	Claudia Bryan Joyce
Prop Maker	Sophie Phillips

WARDROBE

Costume Supervisor	Emma Glover
Costume Assistant & Dresser	India Askem

Hull Truck Theatre is dedicated to delivering exceptional theatre for a diverse audience, including those encountering it for the first time.

As part of our Hull UK City of Culture 2017 programme we're producing work at an unprecedented scale with some of the largest cast sizes ever to grace our stages. We are thrilled to be working with an exceptional range of internationally renowned artists and companies, commissioning writers to produce world premières right here in Hull and working with local people to tell their own unique stories.

We see culture as a powerful regenerative tool for our city, enabling it to meet its ambitions and commitment to overcoming social and economic challenges. We are a pioneering theatre with a contemporary Northern voice, locally rooted, global in outlook, inspiring artists, exciting audiences and supporting communities to reach their greatest potential.

Through our work with schools and with the community, we help to raise aspirations and give life-changing creative opportunities to thousands of young people, disabled groups and adults.

Hull Truck Theatre gratefully acknowledges funding from:

'We believe that everyone has the right to enjoy and be enriched by high quality artistic work that is culturally relevant to people and place. We aim to be a thriving creative organisation that tells extraordinary human stories, offering fresh and imaginative perspectives on the world.'
Mark Babych, Artistic Director

HULL TRUCK THEATRE HISTORY

Hull Truck Theatre tells powerful human stories that resonate with our times.

We have been making theatre for over 45 years, starting with a group of friends in the back of a truck, to a venue on Spring Street, to our purpose-built home on Ferensway.

The company began in 1971 after director Mike Bradwell placed a magazine advert reading 'half-formed theatre company seeks other half'. Various artists responded, moved to Hull and began devising their own plays — Hull Truck Theatre was born. An anarchic spirit and a passion for telling stories were at the heart of the company from the very beginning and brought our performances to national attention.

In the 1980s John Godber took the helm. We moved to our first permanent building, a renovated church hall on Hull's Spring Street, creating a stream of popular hits which toured to great acclaim.

In 2012 we celebrated our 40th anniversary by moving into a new home on Ferensway, and the following year Artistic Director Mark Babych joined to lead the company on the next stage of our journey.

We create exceptional drama which builds on traditions laid down by writers including Anthony Minghella and Alan Plater, as well as creating new work with artists such as James Graham, Tanika Gupta and Bryony Lavery. We make work with local people, programme the very best in live performance and build partnerships with others to create a vibrant and dynamic cultural hub for Hull that is inspiring, creative and welcoming.

HULL
2017
UK
City
of
Culture

HULL UK CITY OF CULTURE 2017

The story so far…

When in 2013 it was announced that Hull was to be UK City of Culture 2017, the city erupted with huge excitement.

It's an award given every four years to a city that demonstrates the belief in the transformative power of culture. Here was an unprecedented opportunity to put Hull on the map and to help build a legacy, positioning it as a place to live, visit, study and invest in.

Culture Company (Hull 2017), established to deliver on that promise, set out to produce 365 days of great art and cultural events inspired by the city and told to the world. The ambition was to create a nationally significant event that celebrates the unique character of Hull, its people and heritage. It offers a programme that takes in every art form, from theatre and performance, to visual arts and literature, to music and film, which goes into every corner of the city, whilst showcasing it nationally.

Working with local as well as national and international artists and cultural institutions, Hull 2017 also draws on the distinctive spirit of the city and the artists, writers, directors, musicians, revolutionaries and thinkers that have made such a significant contribution to the development of art and ideas.

The positive reaction to the programme has exceeded all expectations, with Hull now being taken seriously as a cultural destination for must-see events. The theatre programme for the year is set to continue to challenge and thrill new and existing audiences in the city and beyond, and will set the standard for the quality of work to expect from Hull in the future.

Characters

NADEZHDA
(47 year-old woman)

VERA
(57 year-old woman) – Nadezhda's older sister

NIKOLAI
(84 year-old Ukrainian man)

MIKE
(47 year-old English man) – Nadezhda's husband

VALENTINA
(36 year-old Ukrainian woman) – Nikolai's
young wife

STANISLAV
(14 year-old Ukrainian boy) – Valentina's son

LUDMILLA
(Ukrainian woman in her 30s) – Late mother to
Vera and Nadezhda and 1st wife of Nikolai's

7 main characters

Other characters:

The idea behind this play is to use an ensemble
to dramatise scenes, especially bringing
Ludmilla's past to life – so that all the actors
would be involved in multiple

CHARACTERS

ENSEMBLE WOULD PLAY:

DUBOV, POLICE MAN, SONIA AND MITROFAN
OCHERETKO AND THEIR WEDDING GUESTS,
OLD FRIENDS OF LUDMILLA, THE TSAR, BOB
TURNER, RUSSIAN SOLDIERS, UKRAINIAN
VILLAGERS, WORKMEN, IMMIGRATION
OFFICERS, ERIC PYKE, BALD ED, PSYCHIATRIST,
NIGHBOUR, MAN, COMMUNIST PARTY
OFFICIAL, AUNTY SHURA, YOUNG NIKOLAI,
YOUNG VERA, KISHKA, NAZI OFFICER.

ACT ONE

SCENE 1

A very messy lounge with a kitchen on one side. Wilting, dying pots of herbs line the kitchen window whilst newspapers filled with apple peel litter the floor.

NIKOLAI is sat in a corner of the lounge, head in his hands, in grief.

Enter LUDMILLA, a sprightly young Ukrainian woman carrying a battered old suitcase, wearing a hat and a coat. She looks around the room in disgust.

LUDMILLA: *(Accent.) Vat* (what) a mess!

(To the audience.) It says on my tomb stone:

"Ludmilla Mayevska. Born in 1912 in the Ukraine, beloved wife of Nikolai...

LUDMILLA looks across at NIKOLAI.

...Mother of Vera and Nadezhda. Grandmother of Alice, Alexandra and Anna." The stone mason had trouble getting all the words on. Ha! Just above my grave, there is a beautiful cherry tree and beneath it a wooden bench, where I like to sit sometimes and remember.

As LUDMILLA starts to speak, members of the ensemble cast enter as characters from her story. They take clothes, props etc. out of her suitcase to embody the characters they are portraying.

Ukrainian music.

My mother, Sonia Blazkho was eighteen when she married my father, Mitrofan Ocheretko in the beautiful gold domed Cathedral of St Michael in Kiev.

Enter SONIA and MITROFAN, dressed for their wedding. They look lovingly at each other. LUDMILLA throws rose petals as confetti over the bride and groom. Ukrainian wedding music and dance throughout this description.

1

She wore a white dress and a veil and a pretty gold locket hung around her neck. Her long brown hair was crowned with white flowers. My uncle, her oldest brother Pavel Blazhko, railway engineer, later friend to

Lenin, gave her away. My aunt, her older sister Shura, recently qualified as a doctor, was maid of honour.

> *The Ocheretko men stride in, in their riding boots, embroidered shirts and baggy trousers. The women wear wide swinging skirts and boots with little heels and coloured ribbons in their hair. Everyone drinks vodka.*

ENSEMBLE: Nazdrovya!

> *All dance to Ukrainian wedding music.*

The Blazhkos looked down on my father's family. They said they were uncouth, that they drank too much and never combed their hair. The Ocheretkos thought my mother's family, the Blazhkos, were prissy urbanites.

> *A big fight ensues between the families. Men square up to each other and punches are thrown.*

My mother and father didn't care what their parents thought. They were in love.

> *As SONIA and MITROFAN kiss, they and the rest of the ensemble exit, LUDMILLA is left on her own. She smiles at the memory. She closes her case and places it in the corner of the room.*

LUDMILLA: *(To the audience.)* Without me here – who will remember the stories from before?

> *NADEZDHA enters. It is a sunny day. She takes in the messy room and looks disheartened. LUDMILLA looks at her lovingly and then exits.*

LUDMILLA: *(Calls back.)* I go to garden. Try and tidy the weeds.

Terribble state!

NADEZHDA: *(Calls out.)* Pappa! Pappa?

> *NADEZHDA picks up a few clothes off the floor and folds them up. She picks up the bin liner LUDMILLA was*

> *using and continues her work of clearing the place up.*
> *NIKOLAI enters, looking shabby, he is carrying a pyrex*
> *dish with apples in it.*

NIKOLAI: Nadezhda!

NADEZHDA: Pappa! Look at this place! It's such a mess.

> *NIKOLAI looks around the room surprised.*

NADEZHDA: What have you there?

NIKOLAI: I am going to make you a delicious dessert.

NADEZHDA: You're cooking?

NIKOLAI: Don't look so surprised. Toshiba apples.

> *NIKOLAI opens a microwave and pops the pyrex dish*
> *in there. He presses a few buttons and the microwave*
> *buzzes into life.*

NIKOLAI: Ready in just a few moments. How was your drive?

NADEZHDA: Not so bad.

> *NIKOLAI briefly hugs NADEZHDA in greeting. It is an*
> *awkward hug.*

NADEZHDA: What's so urgent? You said you wanted to talk to me about something?

NIKOLAI: Yes. Important.

> *NIKOLAI notes NADEZHDA's look of worry.*

NIKOLAI: Nothing to worry about. Sit! Sit!

> *NADEZHDA looks worried nevertheless.*

NADEZHDA: Shall I make us some tea?

NIKOLAI: Tea later. First my good news.

NADEZHDA: Go on.

NIKOLAI: Nadezhda! I'm getting married.

> *NADEZHDA is speechless.*

NIKOLAI: She is coming with her son from Ukrainia. Ternopil in Ukrainia.

NADEZHDA is silent, staring at her father in amazement.
VALENTINA enters with a pink, fluffy suitcase. She walks
in lazily and sexily and stands between them both. She
is a big, busty, beautiful, brunette woman.

VALENTINA: Valentina, but I am more like Botticelli's Venus
rising from the waves. Luscious hair. Charming eyes.

NIKOLAI: Superior breasts.

VALENTINA: When you see me, you will understand.

BEAT as NADEZHDA tries hard not to overreact.

NADEZHDA: When can I meet her?

NIKOLAI: After marriage you can meet.

NADEZHDA: I think it might be better if we could meet her
first, don't you?

NIKOLAI: Why you want to meet? You not marrying her.

NADEZHDA: How old is she?

VALENTINA: Thirty-six.

NADEZHDA: And you are –

VALENTINA: Eighty-four

NIKOLAI: So *vat?* (what)

NADEZHDA: It's quite an age difference.

NIKOLAI: So *vat?* Nadezhda. I had no idea you were so bourgeois!

NADEZHDA: No, it's just there could be problems.

NIKOLAI: There will be no problems. I have anticipated all
problems.

NADEZHDA: How long have you known her?

VALENTINA: Three months.

NADEZHDA: Not very long.

NIKOLAI: She has an uncle in Selby – is coming to visit him
on a tourist visa.

A young boy – STANISLAV enters and stands next to VALENTINA. He looks like a typical sulky teenager. He is eating his way through a packet of biscuits.

VALENTINA: I want make a new life for myself and my son in the West, a good life, with good job, good money, nice car.

STANISLAV: Absolutely no Lada no Skoda –

VALENTINA: Good education for son.

STANISLAV: Must be Oxford Cambridge.

VALENTINA: Nothing less.

NADEZHDA: Pappa...

VALENTINA: I am educated woman by the way.

NIKOLAI: She has a diploma in pharmacy. She will easily find well-paid work here. In the meantime, I am helping her with her English and she is cleaning house and looking after me.

NADEZHDA looks around the messy house bemused.

NIKOLAI: She sits on my lap and allows me to fondle her breasts.

VALENTINA: We are happy together.

NADEZHDA bolts up from her chair and walks away, trying to hide her horror. NIKOLAI continues to chatter, excited by his plans.

NIKOLAI: I will put a roof over her head.

VALENTINA: And I will look after my *holubchik* as he gets older.

NIKOLAI: Share my pension until she gets work.

NADEZHDA: Your tiny pension?

VALENTINA: My son is extraordinarily gifted boy.

STANSILAV: I am genius – play piano – will get an English education.

NIKOLAI: We will discuss art, literature, philosophy together in the evenings.

VALENTINA: I am cultured woman, not chatterbox peasant type.

5

NIKOLAI: I have already elicited her views on Nietzsche and Schopenhauer, by the way, and she agrees with me in all respects.

NADEZHDA: How convenient!

NIKOLAI: She, like me, admires Constructivist art and hates neo-classicism.

VALENTINA: I hate neo-classicism.

STANISLAV: Hate it.

NIKOLAI: We have much in common. A sound foundation for marriage.

NADEZHDA: But Pappa! Wouldn't she be better off with someone her own age? The authorities will know it's a marriage of convenience. They're not stupid. She could be sent back.

VALENTINA throws NADEZHDA a death stare.

NADEZHDA: You haven't thought this through.

NIKOLAI: I am Valentina's last hope! I am her only chance to escape a life of persecution...

VALENTINA: ... destitution.

STANISLAV: ...Prostitution!

VALENTINA gives STANISLAV a hard stare.

NIKOLAI: Life in the Ukraine is too hard for such a delicate spirit as hers.

NADEZHDA: What do your friends say about this?

VALENTINA: He has no friends.

NADEZHDA: The community! Your fellow Ukrainians, mother's friends, neighbours...

A couple of the ENSEMBLE become the disapproving neighbours.

VALENTINA: Pah! They are all too narrow minded.

ENSEMBLE: We are not impressed with her views on Nietzsche.

VALENTINA: They are bound up in the past, Ukrainian nationalists – all of them!

NADEZHDA: So, they don't like Valentina?

VALENTINA: I, modern, liberated woman. They spread vile rumours.

NADEZHDA: What do they say?

ENSEMBLE: She sold her mother's goat and cow to buy grease to put on her face to attract Western men.

VALENTINA: They speak rubbish. My mother had chickens and pigs – she never had goat or cow.

NIKOLAI: Just goes to show how foolish they are!

NADEZHDA: Pappa, maybe you should listen to them. You've known your friends around here your whole life – certainly longer than three months.

NIKOLAI: I disown them all! I tell them to get lost! I don't need their advice.

NADEZHDA: Pappa...

NIKOLAI: If needs be, I will disown my daughters. I will stand alone against the world – alone apart from the beautiful woman by my side.

VALENTINA tickles NIKOLAI under the chin.

VALENTINA: *Holubchik.*

NADEZHDA is silent. She starts to tidy up the room.

NIKOLAI: And one more thing, Nadia. Don't tell that sister of yours.

NADEZHDA: You haven't told Vera?

VERA enters.

VERA: Told me what?

NADEZHDA: I haven't spoken to her in two years – not since mother's funeral.

At the mention of 'mother' the two of them fall silent for a moment.

7

NIKOLAI: It's Vera's fault your mother died.

VERA: Here we go…

NIKOLAI: All that moaning she did about her divorce. She poisoned her mind with her words.

NADEZHDA: *(Gently.)* It was cancer Pappa. You know that it wasn't Vera. Why do you hate her so much?

NIKOLAI: Vera, she is a tyrant. Like Stalin. Always pestering me. Must do this, must do that.

VERA: Pappa, you belong in a Home. Nadezhda, this is all your fault.

VERA exits.

NADEZHDA: Is this whole marriage business because you're lonely Pappa? I keep telling you that Mike and I both agree –

MIKE steps forward.

MIKE: Nikolai, we've said often enough – you can come and live with us. You're aways welcome.

NIKOLAI: Thank you – but I must decline because –

I am in love.

NADEZHDA & MIKE: Really?

NIKOLAI: Yes. Really! But there is a small problem. Valentina must still get divorce papers from her husband.

NADEZHDA: She's married to someone else?

VALENTINA: My husband is very intelligent type, Polytechnic director.

DUBOV enters, he stands and smiles at everyone.

NIKOLAI: I have been in correspondence with him – even spoke to him on the telephone.

DUBOV: Valentina will make excellent wife.

VALENTINA: You see?

VALENTINA pats DUBOV on the head. He smiles and nods.

NADEZHDA: Are you mad Pappa?

NIKOLAI: Nadezhda, you have to understand that in some respects the man is governed by different impulses to the woman.

NADEZHDA: Pappa, please spare me the biological determinism.

NIKOLAI: Tell me Nadezhda, do you think it would be possible for a man of eighty-four to father a child?

NADEZHDA looks at her father in abject horror.

NIKOLAI: You see I am thinking that if she is a mother to the British citizen as well as wife of British citizen, they surely won't be able to deport her.

NADEZHDA: Pappa, just stop and think for a minute. Is this really what you want?

ENSEMBLE: *Tak!*

NIKOLAI: Technically it may be possible…snag is, hydraulic lift no longer fully functioning. But maybe with Valentina…what do you think?

NADEZHDA can hardly disguise her disgust. The ENSEMBLE all groan.

ENSEMBLE: Ohhhh!

NADEZHDA: Pappa. I don't know what to think.

The microwave pings loudly.

NIKOLAI: Ah! Toshiba apples. Ready! Good. Make tea Nadezhda.

SCENE 2

MIKE and NADEZHDA are dressed in their pyjamas, getting ready for bed – brushing their teeth.

NADEZHDA: I actually think he's mad.

MIKE: He's always been a little eccentric.

NADEZHDA: What should I do Mike? Tell me what to do?

MIKE: Calm down for a start.

NADEZHDA: She's in the country.

MIKE: Valentina – nice name – has a certain romantic ring to it...

NADEZHDA: Mike!

MIKE laughs.

NADEZHDA: This is a really serious matter. Pappa is about to be taken to the cleaners by an opportunist Ukrainian harlot!

MIKE: Nadezhda...

NADEZHDA: He's eighty-four! What woman in her right mind, would want to marry him! I'd understand it if it was a local widowed neighbour – his age – or nearabouts, but she's thirty-six!

MIKE: Is she staying with him?

NADEZHDA: No. Apparently she's with her 'uncle' in Selby.

MIKE: He didn't say anything last weekend when we saw him.

NADEZHDA: No, but he was acting strangely wasn't he?

MIKE: He seemed happy, excited.

NADEZHDA: Very suspicious.

MIKE: It's the testosterone surge. His back's straightened up and his arthritis is better.

MIKE laughs.

NADEZHDA: You men, you think sex is the cure for everything.

MIKE: It cures quite a lot of things.

MIKE puts his arms around NADEZHDA and nuzzles her but NADEZHDA is irritated and pushes MIKE away.

NADEZHDA: When I tell my girlfriends about this business, they're absolutely appalled. They see a vulnerable old man being exploited. But all the men I talk to – you included – respond with these wry knowing smiles, admiring laughs. What a lad! What a young, sexy bird. Go for it Nikolai! Have some fun!

MIKE: Admit it. It's done him good.

NADEZHDA: Rubbish

MIKE: If you're that worried, you should phone your sister. *He might listen to her.*

NADEZHDA: Are you joking? He hates her.

MIKE: 'Hate's' a bit strong. Shame they don't get on – never understood why?

NADEZHDA: Who knows?

MIKE: Phone Vera.

NADEZHDA: No!

MIKE fetches the phone and holds it out to NADEZHDA.

MIKE: Phone her.

NADEZHDA: He's behaving like a horny adolescent.

MIKE: You're being puritanical.

NADEZHDA: And you're encouraging him.

MIKE: No I'm not.

NADEZHDA: Nudge nudge – wink-wink.

MIKE: Give me a break Nadezhda – you're being totally ridiculous. And unfair!

NADEZHDA: Am I?

MIKE: You're never too old for love.

NADEZHDA: You mean sex.

MIKE: That as well. Your dad is just fulfilling every man's dream – to be in the arms of a beautiful younger woman.

NADEZHDA leaves the room swiftly. MIKE realizes his faux pas and cringes.

MIKE: *(Calls out.)* I'm sorry, I didn't mean it the way it…it came out wrong…when I said *every* man, I meant…

NADEZHDA re enters angrily carrying some pillows and a sleeping bag. She slams them into MIKE's hands.

MIKE: Nadezhda … sweetheart…please…no…

NADEZHDA: Do make yourself comfortable on the couch tonight.

MIKE looks forlornly down at the sleeping bag.

MIKE: *(Whines.)* This sleeping bag – it's so old and scratchy…

NADEZHDA: Sweet dreams Mike. With any luck, you'll be lying in the arms of a beautiful young woman tonight.

MIKE realizes that there's no getting around NADEZHDA. He exits, head hanging low.

NADEZHDA stares at the phone. She paces, annoyed. Eventually, she picks up the phone. This is a hard call to make. She thinks a bit more and then puts the phone down. She can't make the call.

SCENE 3

NIKOLAI's LOUNGE

On one side of the room, NIKOLAI is busy sorting through his papers and marking something up in chalk on the floor. LUDMILLA enters with some flowers and places them in a vase. NADEZHDA enters and starts chopping up vegetables in the kitchen area and putting them into a large saucepan of boiling water.

LUDMILLA: *(To NADEZHDA.)* See? My beautiful roses are still growing in my garden. Every year, they bloom without fail. Why? Because I feed them with special black chocolate. All my vegetables, my herbs and fruit grow in abundance so we will never go hungry.

Did I tell you how my Pappa was awarded the St George's Cross? Pappa – Mitrofan Ocheretko was a brilliant soldier. He loved life but respected death. Unlike officers from the nobility, who didn't even think of the peasants as human, he was careful with his troops' lives, only taking risks when there something to be gained. In 1916, on the Eastern Front, he took a bullet in his thigh at Lake Naroch crawling through a bog to rescue the Tsar's cousin, who had become trapped. My father dragged the young aristocrat to safety and carried him in his arms through gunfire. The Tsar

12

himself pinned the St George's cross on my Pappa's chest and the Tsarina patted me on the head. I was just four years old but I can remember the day.

Two years later, the Tsar and the Tsarina were dead and Pappa was an outlaw on the run.

LUDMILLA looks across at NIKOLAI who is now using chalk on the floor to draw something.

LUDMILLA: I have known ideology and I have known hunger. When I was twenty-one, Stalin discovered he could use famine as a political weapon against the Kulaks. I still see hunger prowling with his skeletal body and gaping eyes, behind the shelves of the supermarket, waiting to grab you the moment you're off guard. He'll shove you on a train, or a cart and send you off on another journey where the end is always death.

NADEZHDA: *(Calls out.)* Pappa! Pappa! What time will Valentina be here?

NIKOLAI: *(Calls back.)* Soon. She said she would come straight after her work.

NADEZHDA: *(Calls out.)* I'm making a special vegetable soup – just like Mum used to. Hope she likes it.

NIKOLAI: *(Calls back.)* Very good.

LUDMILLA and NADEZHDA look into the pot of boiling vegetables.

LUDMILLA: Nadezhda, I will show you how to make the dumplings for the vegetable soup – *halushki* – you make a paste with raw eggs and semolina, salt and herbs which fluff up so it crumbles on your tongue.

MIKE enters from the garden carrying some veg. He hands them to NADEZHDA and kisses her lightly.

MIKE: It's pretty overgrown and wild out there – flowers everywhere but I managed to dig out some potatoes and onions. As for your mum's vegetable patch…the broad beans have rotted and the runner beans are out of control.

NADEZHDA: Any herbs? She had a forest of parsley and dill.

MIKE: Sorry. The weeds have taken over.

MIKE pours three glasses of wine from a bottle.

MIKE: What can I do? Shall I chop for you?

NADEZHDA: No. Please try and talk some sense into Pappa.

MIKE: I'll try, but he is a man possessed.

NADEZHDA: By a demon.

MIKE takes a sip of the wine.

MIKE: This plum wine of your mum's still tastes good…and strong. It's been maturing. There's litres of it left in the shed.

NIKOLAI: *(Calls out.)* Mikhael, I have something important to share with you.

MIKE walks across to NIKOLAI and hands him a glass of plum wine. MIKE looks at the floor.

MIKE: What's all this?

NIKOLAI: I am drawing historical map of Ukraine on the floor.

MIKE: Ahhh…

NIKOLAI: I have done the research. You see Fowler invented the first tractor and saw it as a means to emancipate the laboring masses from their lives of mindless toil. Now I am writing.

MIKE: Your great work?

NIKOLAI: And I have a title. *'A Short History of Tractors in Ukrainian.'* You like it?

MIKE: Very catchy.

NIKOLAI: Also, I have translated it into English, so you can read it. Nadezhda has to help me with some phrases but you can tell me if I am going in the right way with the language.

MIKE: I'd be delighted to.

NIKOLAI: I am poet engineer. I published my first poem when I was just fourteen years old.

MIKE: You were chasing the girls even then?

NIKOLAI: Actually, that was a eulogy to a new hydro-electric Power station built in 1927 on the river Dnieper.

> *MIKE looks surprised. As MIKE settles down in a chair with his plum wine, the ENSEMBLE enters to join in with NIKOLAI's first installment of* 'A Short History of Tractors in Ukrainian'.

POEM 1

NIKOLAI:

John Fowler was a true benefactor
Giving humanity its very first tractor,
A head so clear, the mind of a genius
Thanks to being so abstemious:
No vodka, no wine, no tea and no beer
A Quaker – hardline – and an engineer.

John Fowler worked in anticipation
Of the labouring masses' emancipation
Freeing them from the mindless toil
Of endlessly poughing heavy soil.
Inventing his bizarre contraption
Was an act of deep compassion.

Fowler placed engines either end of a field
And looped a cable around heavy wheels;
On the cable were the blades of a plough
So as engines turned they dug a furrow.
Fowler must have been euphoric –
Such a revolution, so historic.

Thus begins my epic arcadian …
A short history of tractors in Ukranian.

MIKE: *(Applauding.)* Bravo!

NIKOLAI: You like?

ENSEMBLE: We like!

NIKOLAI: Good…

MIKE: But for now, what I really want to know is – when will we get a chance to meet this Goddess of yours Nikolai?

NIKOLAI: She will come when her shift finishes and I have something to give her.

NIKOLAI produces a stuffed brown envelope from his pocket.

MIKE: What's in there?

NIKOLAI: Some of my love poetry.

MIKE: You old rascal Nikolai!

They chink glasses. NIKOLAI beckons MIKE forward to speak to him out of NADEZHDA's earshot.

NIKOLAI: I can understand that Vera and Nadia are not happy. They have lost their mother. But they will come to accept Valentina.

MIKE: So you keep saying Nikolai.

NIKOLAI: You see Mikhail. A child can only have one mother, but a man can have many lovers. This is perfectly normal, agree?

MIKE: Yes, but why Valentina?

NADEZHDA looks across at MIKE to try and eavesdrop, but the men are conspiratorial. The ensemble join in the next section:

NIKOLAI: The talk about Ukraine is of…

STANISLAV: No food in shops;

NIKOLAI: The *hrivna* has fallen through the floor and keeps falling every day and there has been an outbreak of cholera in Kharkiv whilst…

ENSEMBLE: Diptheria is sweeping through the Dombass.

ENSEMBLE: In Chernigov, trees from the forests around Chernobyl have been felled and turned into radioactive furniture.

ENSEMBLE: Which has been sold all around the country so that people are irradiated in their own homes.

NIKOLAI: Can you imagine!

MIKE: No, I don't think I can.

ENSEMBLE: Fourteen miners were killed in an explosion in Donetsk.

ENSEMBLE: And a man was arrested at the railway at Odessa and found to have a lump of uranium in his suitcase.

ENSEMBLE: There is a collapse of law and order and of moral and rational principles.

NIKOLAI: If I can save just one human being from this horror, do you not think this is the moral thing to do?

MIKE: Very noble of you...

NIKOLAI: It is a terrible tragedy what has happened to my beautiful country. The twin evils of fascism and communism have eaten her heart.

> *The phone rings and NIKOLAI gets up to answer it, leaving the brown envelope on the armchair where he was sat. As he is on the phone, NADEZHDA approaches the armchair and picks up the brown envelope. MIKE shoots her a warning look but then looks worried when he sees that it is stuffed full of money. NIKOLAI returns, looking distressed – NADEZHDA turns away as she counts the money.*

NIKOLAI: Valentina...she is...

MIKE: What's wrong Nikolai?

> *NIKOLAI is agitated and paces, muttering under his breath.*

NIKOLAI: Disaster! Not coming...going home!

MIKE: Valentina's not coming after all?

NIKOLAI: She travels back to Ukraine tomorrow. I must see her! I must give her my gift.

> *NADEZHDA holds up the brown envelope accusingly.*

NADEZHDA: This?

NIKOLAI: Yes! Yes – my poems for her.

NADEZHDA: Quite a lot of money in here. Eighteen hundred pounds to be exact.

NIKOLAI chases NADEZHDA as she dances away from him, waving the envelope in the air. He seems desperate.

NADEZHDA: Pappa – why are you giving her money? This must be most of your savings! You're a pensioner – you can't afford it.

NIKOLAI gives chase and finally manages to snatch the envelope back out of NADEZHDA's hands.

NIKOLAI: None of your business. Why you so bothered what I do with my money? You thinking there will be nothing left for you? Ha!

NADEZHDA: She's conning you Pappa. Mike, we should go to the Police.

NIKOLAI yelps, terrified at the mention of Police.

NIKOLAI: Why are you so cruel Nadezhda? How have I raised such a hard hearted monster? Leave my house. I never want to see you again. You are not my daughter.

NIKOLAI starts to cough uncontrollably.

NADEZHDA: Oh stop being so melodramatic Pappa. You said that to me before – do you remember? When I was a student and you thought I was too left wing?

NIKOLAI: Even Lenin wrote that left wing communism is infantile. 'Infantile Disorder.'

NADEZHDA: *(To MIKE.)* He accused me of being a Trotskyist 'Leave my house. I never want to see you again!'

(To NIKOLAI.) But look, I'm still here. Still putting up with your crap.

NIKOLAI: You *were* Trotskyist. All of you student revolutionaries with your stupid flags and banners. Do you know what that monster Trotsky did? Trotsky was evil – worse than Lenin. Worse even than your sister Vera.

MIKE: Come on Nikolai, I'm sure you didn't mean that and Nadezhda, stop raking over arguments from over thirty years ago! Sit down, both of you and let's talk about it.

NIKOLAI listens to MIKE and sits down, but he is shaking. NADEZHDA eyes him with anger and remains standing. MIKE gives her a look which makes her sit down.

MIKE: Nikolai, I think Nadezhda has a point. It's one thing to help Valentina come to England, but it's another thing if she's asking you for money.

NIKOLAI: It's for her tickets. If she is to come back, she needs money for her tickets.

MIKE: But if she really cares about you, she'll come and see you before she goes, won't she? She'll want to say goodbye.

NIKOLAI: Hmmm...

MIKE: I mean it's understandable that you should feel attracted to Valentina...

NADEZHDA gasps with indignation but MIKE gestures at her to be quiet.

MIKE: But I think it's a bit suspicious that she doesn't want to meet your family if she's really thinking of marrying you.

NIKOLAI: Hmm.

MIKE: ...What about the money she is earning? That should be enough?

NIKOLAI: She has debts to pay. If I don't give her money, maybe she will never come back. And my poems...I want her to read them.

NIKOLAI looks lost. NADEZHDA and MIKE exchange a knowing look.

NADEZHDA: There's no fool like an old fool.

NIKOLAI: *(Shouts.)* I am not old!

NADEZHDA: You're eighty-four Pappa.

NIKOLAI: But my heart is still young.

19

MIKE: Where does she stay in Peterborough? Maybe we could call 'round at her house?

SCENE 5

We are outside. We hear the sound of a car draw up and stop (OS). Doors open and are slammed shut.

MIKE: *(Off stage.)* Is this the house?

NIKOLAI: Yes, yes...here...

> *NIKOLAI rushes forward to the front of Stage and looks up.*

NIKIOLAI: *(Calls up.)* Valentina! Valentina! My love! My Holubchik!

> *NADEZHDA and MIKE approach and stand behind NIKOLAI looking up at the house.*

NADEZHDA: Is she in?

NIKOLAI: *(Calls out again.)* Valentina! It is me! Nikolai. Come out so I can give you something before you go back.

> *NIKOLAI holds out his arms in entreaty, waving the brown envelope.*

NIKOLAI: Look what I have for you!

> *MIKE, NADEZHDA and NIKOLAI all look up, expectantly, holding their breath.*

NADEZHDA: The curtains are twitching.

NIKOLAI: *(Calls out.)* That's it my love – don't be shy.

> *We hear the sound of a sash window being pulled up.*

NIKOLAI: Valentina!

> *But instead of VALENTINA, we see a bare chested man appear at the window above (BOB TURNER). He shouts down at NIKOLAI.*

BOB TURNER: OY! PISS OFF WILL YOU? JUST PISS OFF!

NADEZHDA: Who's that?

BOB TURNER: *(Off stage.)* Don't you think you've caused enough trouble already? Pestering her at work, now following her home. You've upset her. Fuck off and leave her alone!

The window slams shut and NIKOLAI looks distraught.

MIKE: I think you've had a lucky escape there.

NIKOLAI is speechless and upset.

NIKOLAI: I will have nothing more to do with her. Let's go home.

NIKOLAI strides off.

MIKE shrugs, smiles apologetically and follows NIKOLAI. NADEZHDA hangs back and continues to stare up at the house, intrigued and confused.

LUDMILLA enters and joins NADEZHDA as they stand together on their own.

LUDMILLA takes NADEZHDA's face in her hands and speaks to her with urgency.

LUDMILLA: Now I am gone Nadezhda – you must look after your Pappa because he is a very foolish man. No common sense at all.

LUDMILLA exits leaving NADEZHDA standing till looking up at the house anxiously.

SCENE 6

NADEZHDA is in her bedroom. MIKE is asleep beside her. She picks up the phone and after a beat, she dials a number. VERA walks in to the other side of the stage as her phone rings. She is dressed in a silk negligee, her hair up in a towel and is smoking a cigarette. VERA picks up a phone.

VERA: Hello?

NADEZHDA: Vera, it's me.

Beat. MIKE lifts his head and peers at NADEZHDA.

MIKE: Finally!

VERA: Have you broken your two year silence to fling more mud at me? Because if you have Nadezhda, I shall simply...

NADEZHDA: No. It's not about Mum's locket. It's Pappa.

VERA: What has the old weasel done now?

NADEZHDA: The place is a mess. He eats tinned food and makes this awful apple slop in the microwave...

VERA: He really should be in sheltered accommodation. I told you – but you wouldn't listen.

NADEZHDA: Vera – he's planning to marry.

VERA laughs.

VERA: Don't be silly. Who'd want to marry that old fool? He's ancient, virtually a fossil.

NADEZHDA: He's serious. There's a woman.

VERA: Fantasy!

NADEZHDA: She's called Valentina. She's Ukrainian, with a son and she's thirty-six years old.

VERA: Good God!

NADEZHDA: Vera – We could end up with a step mother younger than us.

VERA: Have you met her?

The ENSEMBLE step in, including VALENTINA and STANISLAV (who is eating).

NADEZHDA: No. But she has superior breasts, which he likes to fondle.

VERA: The dirty old dog!

NADEZHDA: I'm worried she's using Pappa to get British citizenship.

VERA: You think?

VALENTINA: He wants to have a Ukrainian family.

NADEZHDA: He's gone mad.

VERA: You've got to stop her.

NADEZHDA: Why me?

VERA: Because I looked after Mum and it's your turn to take some responsibility.

NADEZHDA: I've tried Vera. That's why I'm calling you. We went to meet her and this half dressed man leaned out the window and told him to –

BOB TURNER: Piss off! –

NADEZHDA: She went back to Ukraine and Pappa said he would have nothing more to do. But then...

VERA: What?

VALENTINA: We make up. He send me money for coach tickets for me and Stanislav from Lviv to Ramsgate.

VERA: Whose Stanislav?

STANISLAV: I'm Stanislav.

NADEZHDA: And then she told him she needed extra money.

VALENTINA: For Austrian transit visa.

ENSEMBLE: *(Shouts.)* She's bleeding him dry!

> *MIKE groans in bed. NADEZHDA gets up and paces as she talks.*
>
> *NIKOLAI steps forward, also in his pyjamas, which look a bit tatty. He is also on the phone.*

NIKOLAI: Not only have I rescued this beautiful destitute woman, but I am also in a position to foster the talents of her extraordinarily gifted son.

NADEZHDA: Listen to what else he's done.

VALENTINA: Stanislav is only fourteen but he has been to see independent psychologist, who for small fee...

NADEZHDA: Which of course he paid!

> *VALENTINA produces a certificate and waves it victoriously.*

VALENTINA: ...tested his IQ and written certificate declaring him to be –

STANISLAV: Genius.

NADEZHDA: Of course.

NIKOLAI: This boy is a gifted musician and has been offered a place at a vey prestigious school in Peterborough. Grantminister.

VERA: The private school?

VALENTINA: Of course he is much too intelligent for state school, which is only fit for sons and daughters of farm labourers.

NADEZHDA: *(Furious.)* But we went to the local comp! My daughter went to the local comp.

MIKE covers his head with a pillow.

VERA: Outrageous. I may have sent my girls to private school, but at least it was Dick's hard earned money.

NADEZHDA: How can Pappa afford it?

STANISLAV: He has money.

VERA: I don't know. Maybe she has another benefactor somewhere. BIMBO!

NADEZHDA: CHEAP TART!

VERA: SLUT!

NADEZHDA: BITCH!

MIKE sits up in bed, outraged.

MIKE: I don't recognize you Nadezhda!

NADEZHDA: We're talking about Valentina.

MIKE: Who you haven't even met!

NADEZHDA: Go back to sleep Mike.

Vera, they're definitely going ahead with the wedding. He's really serious about her. Maybe she makes him happy.

VERA: Nadia! So gullible. We read about these people in the papers everyday. Immigrants, asylum seekers, economic migrants. Call them what you will, it's always the most determined and ruthless people who make it over here, and when they find it isn't so easy to get a good job, they will turn to crime.

NADEZHDA: Vera! Listen to yourself.

VERA: Can't you see what will happen if she comes and stays? We've simply got to stop this wedding.

NADEZHDA: He's so determined – I'm not sure we can stop her.

VERA: But what about this man at the window? The one who told Pappa to –

BOB TURNER: Piss off!

VERA: Didn't that put Pappa off?

A bare chested BOB TURNER enters.

BOB TURNER: Hi. I'm Bob Turner.

NIKOLAI: A very decent type.

BOB TURNER: I'm a civil engineer.

VERA: He knows him?

VALENTINA: I explain everything.

NIKOLAI: Valentina and I are friends now – speak on the phone all the time.

VALENTINA: I fuck Bob Turner.

BOB TURNER and VALENTINA blow kisses at each other.

VERA: Doesn't Pappa care?

BOB TURNER: I'd marry Valentina in a flash.

VALENTINA: But his wife no agree divorce.

BOB TURNER: Sorry love. Wife's got me by the short and curlies. She's gone apeshit at me.

NIKOLAI: So Valentina has finished that relationship now.

BOB TURNER looks surprised.

VERA: Of course it's not finished! Can't you see he's being taken for a ride? Or are you as stupid as Pappa?

NADEZHDA: Vera, I'm not stupid. I'm reporting back to you how Pappa is presenting the facts, so that you can see for yourself how deluded he is.

NIKOLAI: This intelligent Bob Turner has paid for my naturalization.

BOB TURNER: It's the least I could do.

NIKOLAI: So that when I marry Valentina, I will be a British subject.

VERA: Oh – my – God.

> BOB TURNER blows more kisses to VALENTINA and exits.

NADEZHDA: What are we going to do? Pappa's being manipulated on all sides.

VERA: We don't want someone so common to carry our name.

NADEZHDA: Come on Vera, our family is not uncommon. We're just an ordinary family, like everybody else.

VERA: We've come from solid bourgeois people Nadezhda, not *arrivistes*

NADEZHDA: But the Ocheretkos were wealthy peasants... hard drinking Cossacks...

VERA: Farmers.

NADEZHDA: Horse dealers.

VERA: Horse *breeders* who supplied horses to the Tsars army.

NIKOLAI: The Mayevskyjs were teachers and your grandfather Mayevskyj was Minister of Education.

NADEZHDA: But only for six months and of a country that didn't really exist.

VERA: Really, Nadia, why must you take such a downbeat view of everything?

NADEZHDA: No, but...

VERA: When I was a little girl, Baba Sonia used to tell us the story of her wedding. Do you remember?

NADEZHDA: Of course I don't! I wasn't born.

VERA: Now that's what a wedding should be like, not this pitiful charade that our father is being dragged through.

NADEZHDA: Look at the dates Vera, our grandmother was four months pregnant.

Music. LUDMILLA enters.

LUDMILLA: They were in love. It was pulled down in 1935.

NADEZHDA: What was?

LUDMILLA: St Michael of the Golden Domes.

NADEZHDA: Who pulled it down?

LUDMILLA: The Russians of course.

VERA: Don't tell Pappa, but I'm going to phone the Home Office about Valentina being a bogus visa seeker.

NADEZHDA: *(Shocked.)* Vera!

NADEZHDA looks at MIKE to check he can't hear.

VERA: This gold digging, brunette bombshell, with her superior breasts is not going to con our father of his small worldly possessions. In the memory of our long suffering mother who worked and suffered all her life, scrimping and saving, chasing away the threat of starvation, growing her own food to put dinner on our plates, we will not allow this interloper to step into her shoes and squander what our mother worked so hard for.

We have to use all means necessary to stop her.

ENSEMBLE cheer.

NADEZHDA: But writing to the Home Office… It's a step too far.

MIKE sits up in bed. He tries to listen in to the conversation.

VERA: Let me call the British Embassy in Kiev. If we can get them to refuse her a British visa, then we're well shot of Valentina.

NADEZHDA: I don't even know when they're planning this wedding.

NIKOLAI: You are not invited. It is a small affair. You have shown you are not willing to wish me well. I understand.

VALENTINA: No need to be there.

NADEZHDA: When?

NIKOLAI: It is not certain.

VERA: So you're not getting married?

NIKOLAI: I have paid £500 for the wedding dress. £100 for the photographer. We need professional photos for the immigration officials.

> *VALENTINA pulls a wedding dress out of the suitcase and gets dressed.*

NADEZHDA: Did he ever love Mum?

NIKOLAI and VALENTINA: Ah love! What thing is love? No one can understand.

NIKOLAI: On this point, science must concede to poetry.

NADEZHDA: I managed to get him to admit that they're getting married at the Church of The Immaculate Conception.

VERA: But Pappa's an atheist.

VALENTINA: I am a Catholic.

NIKOLAI: I am humouring her. It is natural for women to be irrational.

VERA: I must go and see him – This is madness!

NIKOLAI: No need to visit now. Everything is okay.

NADEZHDA: We should go to the wedding.

NIKOLAI: No. You can come after June 1st.

NADEZHDA: June 1st!

> *NIKOLAI puts down the phone and starts to undress out of his pyjamas and into a suit.*

VERA: Nadezhda, we've got four weeks to stop her.

> *MIKE is irritated by the conversation. He grabs the phone off NADEZHDA.*

MIKE: Hullo Vera, it's Mike.

VERA: Hello Mike – Long time no see.

MIKE: Have either of you considered that maybe it'll be okay? Maybe Valentina'll look after your Pappa and make him happy in his final years? It's better than going into a home.

VERA: You think that sort of a woman will stick around when he's old – dribbling and shitting his pants? She'll take him for everything and then leave.

> *NADEZHDA grabs the phone back off MIKE.*

NADEZHDA: But Vera, you and I aren't going to look after him are we?

VERA: I did what I could for Mum. For Pappa, I just feel a sense of obligation, nothing more.

NADEZHDA: He isn't so easy to love.

> *NIKOLAI fiddles with his tie, knotting and then unknotting it and then he produces a red rose which he sniffs with delight before tucking it into the lapel of his suit.*

VERA: Love's got nothing to do with it. I'll do my duty as I sincerely hope you will too.

NADEZHDA: I couldn't look after him full time Vera. It'd drive me mad. But I want him to be happy.

> *NIKOLAI appraises himself in the mirror, delighted. He likes what he sees and does a quick skip and a jig.*

VERA: I'll phone the Home Office – try and throw a spanner in the works.

NADEZHDA: Vera – I'm not sure…

VERA: Leave it to me.

> *As NADEZHDA and VERA put down their phones, NADEZHDA clambers into bed with MIKE.*

MIKE: You and your sister seem to have made up. But this writing to the Home Office…

NADEZHDA: Vera's idea, not mine.

MIKE: I noticed you didn't try and stop her.

NADEZHDA: If Pappa won't listen to reason…

MIKE: *(Angry.)* You don't know Valentina. She may be desperate to get away because of all sorts of reasons. What gives you the right?

NADEZHDA: Mike…she's taking advatntage of my elderly father!

MIKE: You were an immigrant once.

NADEZHDA: That's completely different.

MIKE: Is it?

MIKE turns over in bed and switches off the light.

NADEZHDA: *(A voice in the dark.)* How could he just forget her like this? They were married for sixty years.

We hear wedding music as STANISLAV enters, also suited and walks somberly up to NIKOLAI. He stands by his side, but not too close. VALENTINA now dressed in her low cut wedding dress, clutching a bouquet of flowers. NIKOLAI cannot hide his excitement which brims over into nervous giggling as she stands by him with the same bored look she had earlier. As the wedding music stops, VALENTINA bends down to allow NIKOLAI to kiss her. He tries a full frontal attack on the lips, but she turns her face away and instead kisses him on the cheek.

NIKOLAI smiles away his disappointment as STANISLAV throws confetti over the two. A photographer enters and takes lots of shots. VALENTINA directs him carefully as to which photo montages she wants.

They exit, arm in arm, smiling and waving.

SCENE 6

LUDMILLA'S GRAVE.

LUDMILLA enters and sweeps up the confetti as NADEZHDA enters with some flowers. She tidies the grave and then sits under the cherry tree in troubled contemplation.

Music as the ensemble company enter.

SONIA and MITROFAN, now with children dance together.

LUDMILLA: After the revolution of 1917, my Pappa went off to fight with the Ukrainian National Republicans. He thought that whilst Russia tore itself apart, this was a moment to be seized: Ukraine could slip free.

> *SONIA and MITROFAN part with a heavy heart.*

We went to Poltava and waited. I rarely saw Pappa in those years.

> *LUDMILLA joins in with her siblings as they run and play. SONIA hanging up washing in the back/g.*

My childhood was so happy. The summers were hot and me and my younger sister and brother ran barefoot in the fields, swam naked in the Sula river or we took our cow for long walks to pasture and stayed outdoors til night time. The grass was tall enough to hide in and the sky was blue-blue. The cornfields were like a sheet of gold stretching off into the distance. But sometimes, far away, we could hear shooting and see curls of smoke rising from a burning house.

> *MITROFAN returns exhausted and ragged. SONIA tends to his wounds.*

SOLDIER (O/S): Where is he?

LUDMILLA: In 1930, when I was eighteen, my father was arrested.

> *A SOLDIER enters, aggressive and vicious. He over turns things and shouts.*

SOLDIER: Mitrofan Ocheretko?

> *The children all cry and SONIA gathers them to her protectively.*

SOLDIER: Give him up now and we'll go easy on you and the children.

SONIA: Please, spare him. He's done nothing wrong.

SOLDIER: *(Calls out.)* Mitrofan Ocheretko, you're under arrest and charged with training Ukrainian combatants.

SONIA: No! I beg you – have mercy.

> *MITROFAN appears, sleepy, half dressed. SOLDIER grabs him in an arm lock.*

MITROFAN: Please, you're frightening the children.

SOLDIER: Spawn of a traitor.

MITROFAN: Don't talk about them like that.

> *SOLDIER beats MITROFAN viciously with the butt of his rifle. MITROFAN falls to the floor as SONIA screams alongside the children.*

SONIA: No! Don't hurt him – please.

> *MITROFAN is bleeding as he is hauled up by the soldiers and marched away.*

MITROFAN: *(Calls back.)* Don't worry! Don't cry. I'll be back in the morning.

> *SONIA and the children are traumatized as they all cry.*

CHILDREN: Pappa! Pappa!

SONIA: Don't take him – no! Mitrofan!

LUDMILLA: He was taken to the military prison in Live where he was charged. He never stood trial.

> *SONIA and her children take bundles of food to the prison gates and hand them to SOLDIER who is standing guard. They go back and forth as time passes.*

LUDMILLA: Everyday for six months, me my mother, brother and sister would go to the prison with a bundle of food. We handed it to the guard hoping that at least some of it would get to our Pappa. One day the guard said:

SOLDIER: There's no need to come tomorrow. He won't be needing your food anymore.

SONIA falls to her knees and cries. LUDMILLA helps her mother up and hugs her. SONIA gathers her children around her as they take their belongings and eat under the cherry tree.

LUDMILLA: After my father was executed we went back to the Poltava farm. Very fertile farmland. In the autumn of 1932 the army seized the entire harvest – even the seed for next year's planting was taken. We ate our cows, chickens and goats, then our cats and dogs; then rats and mice, then grass. About ten million people died across Ukraine in the Holodomor, the famine of 1932-1933. Lucky for us, my mother was a survivor. She made watery soup from grass and wild sorrel. She dug for roots of horse radish and found a few potatoes in the garden. When we were too hungry to sleep we sang.

NADEZHDA sings a song with LUDMILLA.

NADEZHDA: *There is a tall hill and beneath it a meadow*
A green meadow, so abundant
You would think you were in paradise

LUDMILLA: In the next village, there was a woman who had eaten her baby. She went mad and wandered through the lanes crying.

MAD WOMAN: But she died first, she was dead. What harm to eat? So plump! Why waste? I didn't kill! No! No! No! She died first.

LUDMILLA takes the broom and exits, leaving NADEZHDA on her own and slightly maudlin.

VALENTINA enters. She is wearing a denim mini skirt now. She carries some flowers and she stops and stares at NADEZHDA who stares back, slightly surprised.

NADEZHDA: Hallo… Valentina?

VALENTINA: Nadezhda.

NADEZHDA: It's nice to meet you at last.

VALENTINA: I bring flowers for your mother, from garden.

NADEZHDA: *(Surprised.)* That's nice of you. She loved those roses.

VALENTINA places the cut flowers on LUDMILLA's grave and crosses herself and kisses her fingertips as she does so.

NADEZHDA: Do you come here a lot?

VALENTINA: No. My first time. I not come again. Hate graveyard. I pay respect.

LUDMILLA watches VALENTINA carefully, taking in her outfit, make up and hair.

VALENTINA: You come for lunch. We go back. I cook.

NADEZHDA: Lovely.

VALENTINA: You like vodka?

NADEZHDA: I'm more of a tea person.

VALENTINA: Hmmm…You very English.

NADEZHDA laughs.

NADEZHDA: I do drink vodka, just not at lunch time.

VALENTINA: I can make tea.

The two of them exit.

SCENE 7

NIKOLAI's HOUSE.

MIKE and NIKOLAI are sat together. NIKOLAI starts to recite his next installment of his tractors eulogy.

POEM 2

NIKOLAI + ENSEMBLE:
John Fowler, the Quaker, deserves absolution
From what followed Russia's revolution;
Stalin and his secretariat
Wanted an urban proletariat,

Industrialisation of the city
Meant rural reforms that were not pretty.

Stalin's solution was to authorize
That all peasants should be collectivized
Field boundaries were removed by force
Through the brutal work of the iron horse
Crudely built with slatted wheels
The tractors heeded no appeals.

Reluctant to see their way of life lapse
Resistance rose from Ukranian kulaks.
Stalin's response was typically ruthless,
(Though propaganda left us truthless):
In the harvest of 1932
He seized all the food Ukrainians grew.

Ukrainia's grain was all transported
And the resulting hunger went unreported.
The cities gorged on Stalin's pillages
Whilst starvation stalked Ukrainian villages.
Hunger used as a political tool
Nothing on earth can be as cruel.

MIKE applauds as VALENTINA re-enters.

MIKE: Well done Nikolai. Your English is perfect!

NADEZHDA: Well done Pappa.

VALENTINA kisses NIKOLAI on the nose.

VALENTINA: *Holubchik!*

(Calls.) Stanislav! Come! Help!
Now we must eat. Food is ready.

MIKE and NADEZHDA pull out the table as STANISLAV
and VALENTINA serve plates.

VALENTINA: Roast meat, gravy and potatoes.

NADEZHDA: You cooked it quickly. Did you prepare it earlier?

VALENTINA: I prepare it in microwave.

MIKE: Excellent. Why bother with all that fussy business?

VALENTINA: I work all day in the nursing home, so I have little time. I make modern cooking, not peasant cooking.

NIKOLAI: Valentina is a good cook.

STANISLAV: And we have ice cream for afterwards.

VALENTINA: Eat dinner first.

> *MIKE tucks in.*

MIKE: Delicious.

> *VALENTINA smiles flirtatiously at MIKE.*

VALENTINA: You good eat. I like man good eat. Why you not eat more Nikolai?

NIKOLAI: Too much food make fatty. You are a little bit fatty Valentina.

VALENTINA: Better fatty than skinny.

NIKOLAI: Nadezhda looks like a starving Bangladesh-lady.

NADEZHDA: Thin is good. Thin is healthy. Thin people live longer.

> *NIKOLAI, VALENTINA and STANISLAV all fall about laughing.*

NIKOLAI: Thin is hunger! Thin is famine!

STANISLAV: Everybody thin drop over dead.

NIKOLAI: I like fatty.

> *He places his hand on VALENTINA's breast and gives it a squeeze. MIKE starts to cough and splutter.*

NADEZHDA: So Valentina, how are you settling in to life here?

VALENTINA: Is okay.

NIKOLAI: We are very happy.

MIKE: And how is school Stanislav?

STANISLAV: My school in Ukraine was better. More discipline, more homework. But now in Ukrainia you have to pay the teachers if you want to pass the exams.

NADEZHDA: No different to your English private school then.

MIKE: *(Coughs.)* No different to the schools here. Our daughter Anna was always having to bribe her teachers with apples.

STANISLAV: Apples?

MIKE: A joke. Don't children in your country give their teachers apples?

STANISLAV: Apples never. Vodka, yes.

VALENTINA: *(To NADEZHDA.)* You in University teacher?

NADEZHDA: Erm...yes.

VALENTINA: I want help for Stanislav in Oxford Cambridge university. You working Cambridge University, so you help?

NADEZHDA: Yes, I work in Cambridge, but not the University. I'm at the Anglia Polytechnic University.

VALENTINA: Angella University? What is this?

> *NIKOLAI bends over and whispers in VALENTINA's ear. She seems to understand and looks at NADEZHDA suspiciously.*

VALENTINA: We need new car to drive Stanislav to school. Must be good car.

NIKOLAI: I saw a nice second hand Ford Fiesta in good condition.

VALENTINA: No Ford Fiesta.

MIKE: What kind of a car did you have in mind?

STANISLAV: Mercedes or Jaguar at least.

> *NIKOLAI starts to cough. VALENTINA hands him a glass of water.*

VALENTINA: Other parents in the school have Range Rovers, Saabs. We must look equal.

NADEZHDA: You have a driving licence?

VALENTINA: I have International drivers licence from Ternopil which is valid for one year.

MIKE: You might have to take a driving test here then.

VALENTINA: Test?

MIKE: You never took a driving test…?

VALENTINA: I pay for licence in pork cutlets from my mother's small holding.

NIKOLAI: In our country, you can buy anything with anything.

VALENTINA: I am good driver but we need car.

NIKOLAI: Yes but…

VALENTINA: Mrs Zadchuk tell me it is the husband's duty to pay for the wife's car.

NADEZHDA: You've become friends with Mrs Zadchuk?

VALENTINA: She is very helpful. Explain how things work here in this country.

NIKOLAI: Ford is a very reputable company. They make good cars.

VALENTINA: Ford is crap car.

STANISLAV: It is crap car.

VALENTINA: Also cooker is crap. Only two of the three rings work and the oven timer is kaput. Also cooker is electric which is not as prestigious as gas.

NADEZHDA: That was Mum's cooker.

VALENTINA: It is thirty years old and it is crap cooker. And I want brown cooker.

NADEZHDA: Brown?

VALENTINA: In former soviet Union all cookers are white. Crap cookers.

NIKOLAI: But everything in the kitchen is white – washing machine white, fridge white, freezer white. What is the point of having a brown cooker?

VALENTINA: Because I am civilized person. Cooker must be gas, must be brown. And another problem, the house is dirty. Two years Nikolai not clean properly and Hoover Junior is not picking up properly. I have seen an advertisement for a civilized person's Hoover. Blue. Cylinder. No pushing about. Just suck, suck, suck. I need new car to drive to work and to drive Stanislav to school.

NADEZHDA: The bus system is very good here.

VALENTINA: You want I travel by public transport?

NADEZHDA: That's what we do.

STANISLAV starts to sniffle.

VALENTINA: See? You have upset my boy.

NIKOLAI: I didn't say anything. It was Nadezhda.

NADEZHDA: There's no point buying a car Pappa can't afford.

VALENTINA: He can afford. He has money in bank. Tell him Nikolai.

NIKOLAI: What?

VALENTINA: Tell him, you will buy *pretijeskiy auto.*

NIKOLAI: We'll see.

They eat in silence and clear their plates. Everyone kisses each other on the cheek and NADEZHDA and MIKE exit.

SCENE 8

VERA enters, in jogging clothes and does some stretches. Then she lights a cigarette and makes a phone call. NADEZHDA picks up.

VERA: Well? What's she like? How was she dressed?

NADEZHDA: Huge tits, push up bra, tight, too tight top, cheap make up, bleached hair with brown roots showing.

VERA: I knew it. He's married a tart!

NADEZHDA: Strange thing.

VERA: What?

NADEZHDA: I met her at Mum's grave. She brought flowers for her.

VERA: Really?

NADEZHDA: She was paying her respects.

VERA: Or maybe she was checking out if Mum really was dead.

> *Back in the lounge, NIKOLAI is sitting surrounded by his books whilst VALENTINA is hoovering around him. He doesn't lift a finger to help, but makes a mess with his papers.*

NADEZHDA: They look absolutely ridiculous together. I try to think well of her Vera, but she's money grabbing.

VERA: Poor Mum.

NADESZHDA: Pappa bought her a Rover. It's shiny and green and drove for a few trips beautifully and then broke down.

VERA: He told me. Apparently the clutch is shot.

NADEZHDA: He asked me for £100 to get it fixed.

VERA: He asked me for £200.

> *VALENTINA stops hoovering and stands in front of NIKOLAI.*

VALENTINA: My sister is coming next week. She wants to see for herself how well I am doing.

NIKOLAI: Very nice.

VALENTINA: She must be picked up by car at Heathrow.

NIKOLAI: We don't have a car that works.

VALENTINA: You no good man. You plenty money – meanie. Promise money. Money sit in bank. Promise car. Crap car.

NIKOLAI: You demand prestigious car. Looks prestigious; doesn't go. Ha, ha!

VALENTINA: Crap car, crap husband.

NIKOLAI: Where you learning this new 'crap' word?

VALENTINA: You engineer. Why you not mending car? Crap engineer.

NIKOLAI: Tell your sister to come by train.

VALENTINA: No.

NIKOLAI: Yes!

VALENTINA: And I want new brown cooker.

NIKOLAI: Brown cooker is too expensive. Nice white one at the co-op.

VALENTINA: You want to give me crap cooker. I cannot cook on that.

NIKOLAI: My wife cooked on that cooker for thirty years, better than your cooking.

> *VALENTINA looms menacingly over NIKOLAI and speaks slowly and threateningly. NIKOLAI cowers.*

VALENTINA: Your wife peasant Baba. Peasant Baba cooking. For civilized person, cooker must be gas, must be brown.

> *VALENTINA wheels the hoover out.*

VERA: And now he's got an astronomical telephone bill. Seven hundred pounds!

> *NIKOLAI picks up the phone.*

NIKOLAI: Can you lend me five hundred pounds?

VERA: Whatever next?

NADEZHDA: Pappa, this has to stop. Why should I pay for her to make phone calls to Ukraine?

NIKOLAI: Not just she. Stanislav also.

> *STANISLAV is making a surreptitious call on the phone, whispering down the line.*

STANISLAV: *(On the phone.)* Pappa! Pappa! It's terrible here. I miss you! The schools are crap, the students are idiots and the teachers oh my God! So lazy!

VERA: He must be firmer with her. They can't just ring up and chat to their friends.

STANISLAV: *(On the phone.)* Pappa! Pappa! Come and get me! The old man is crazy and the whole place smells of rotting apples!

VERA: Valentina should pay for it out of her wages.

STANISLAV: And always fighting. She and the crazy old man – so much shouting. I can't live like this!

NIKOLAI: She doesn't understand, she thinks, everyone in the West is a millionaire. She is not a bad person. She has some incorrect ideas based on Western Propaganda.

VERA: He should tell her if she doesn't pay the bill, the phone will be cut off.

NIKOLAI: Too much talking. Not intelligent talking.

NADEZHDA: He wouldn't mind paying the bill if it was for talking about Nietzsche and Schopenhauer?

VERA and NADEZHDA have a good laugh.

NIKOLAI: She can't pay for the telephone bill because she has to pay for the car.

NADEZHDA: What car?

NIKOLAI: A Lada. She's buying it to take back to Ukraine for her brother.

NADEZHDA: So she has two cars?

VERA: It seems so. Of course these people – they are communists. They've always had everything they wanted, every luxury, every privilege and now they can't rip off the system any more over there, they want to come over here and rip off…

NADEZHDA: It's not quite as simple as that Vera.

VERA: In this country, communists are harmless little people with beards and sandals. But once they get into power suddenly a new vicious type of personality emerges.

NADEZHDA: It's the same people who are always in power – different names, same types.

VERA: I knew you would disagree with me and I really don't want to argue with you about this. You're just going to have to go over there and sort it out.

VERA stubs out her cigarette and hangs up. She jogs off.

NADEZHDA shouts at the phone.

NADEZHDA: Stupid cow!

*The ENSEMBLE, take out the white cooker from the
kitchen and carry in a brown cooker, placing it in the
kitchen. They take the old hoover out and bring in a
Henry Hoover.*

SCENE 9

*STANISLAV is scoffing a large slab of cake and has his head down over
his books. NADEZHDA enters and looks around.*

STANISLAV: Hullo!

NADEZHDA: Working hard Stanislav?

STANISLAV: Maths homework. Boring.

NADEZHDA: Stanislav – what's going on with this car? It
causing a lot of trouble.

STANISLAV: Oh, no trouble. It's all fixed now.

NADEZHDA: But Stanislav, can't you persuade your mother it
would be better to have a smaller car that's more reliable
than this big shiny monster which costs a fortune to run?

STANISLAV: It's okay now. It's a very nice car.

NADEZHDA: But my Pappa can't afford it.

STANISLAV: He has enough money.

VALENTINA enters.

VALENTINA: *(To STANISLAV.)* Stop talk this bad news peeping
no tits crow.

NADEZHDA: Actually, it's you I want to speak to – Valentina.

VALENTINA: *(Suspicious.)* Why?

NADEZHDA: I think you have a misconception of my father's
wealth.

VALENTINA: What you talking? I not understand.

NADEZHDA: Shall we have some tea? Have a nice quiet chat?
Woman to woman?

VALENTINA: *(Even more suspicious.)* I not want tea. I tired. Working all day.

NADEZHDA: Alright then. My Pappa is poor – not rich.

VALENTINA: Before we marry, he write me letters, he tell me he rich. Plenty money in bank.

NADEZHDA: Maybe he didn't tell you the truth.

VALENTINA: He say I can have anything I want.

NADEZHDA: He said those things so you would marry him. Surely you can see that? He's a lonely old man and you're expecting some kind of a millionaire to pay for everything. Aren't you ashamed of yourself?

VALENTINA: You shame. No me shame. You mother die. Now you father marry me. You no like. You make trouble. I understand. I no stupid.

NADEZHDA: I just want you to be kind to him.

VALENTINA: Your Pappa no easy man.

NADEZHDA: I know.

VALENTINA: Your Pappa difficult. Trouble with bath. Trouble with pi-pi and all the time kiss, kiss, touching here, here, here…

> *VALENTINA touches her breasts, thighs and knees.*
> *NADEZHDA looks away.*

VALENTINA: All the time he make trouble for me. Always want oral sex.

NADEZHDA: So why did you come here?

VALENTINA: Why for? For Stanislav. All is for Stanislav. He must have good opportunity. Is no opportunity in Ukrainia. Is only opportunity for gangster prostitute in Ukrainia.

NADEZHDA: Was it better under communism?

VALENTINA: Of course better, was good life. You no understand what type of people is rule country now.

NADEZHDA: But why are you driving around in two cars when Pappa can't afford the repairs? Why are you talking on the telephone to Ukrainia while he's asking me for money to pay the bills?

VALENTINA: He give you money. Now you give him money.

NADEZHDA: You work. You earn money. You should contribute something to the household.

VALENTINA: You father buy me nothing. No car, no jewel, no clothes, no cosmetic, no underclothes!

VALENTINA yanks up her t-shirt displaying her ferocious breasts.

VALENTINA: I buy all! I work, I buy!

NADEZHDA: Pappa is an innocent man. Stupid but innocent. I know what you are and soon enough my Pappa will know.

VALENTINA: Vixen! Crow! You get out my kitchen! Out my house!

NADEZHDA: Not yours – my mother's house!

NIKOLAI enters and sees the two women screaming at each other.

NIKOLAI: Nadezhda, why you poking your nose in here? Not your business.

NADEZHDA: Pappa, you're crazy. First you say Valentina is spending all your money. 'Lend me a hundred pounds, lend me five hundred pounds'. Then you say I shouldn't poke my nose in.

NIKOLAI: I say lend money. I didn't say poke nose in.

NADEZHDA: Pappa, why should I give money for you to spend on the grasping, deceitful, painted bitch?

NIKOLAI: Get out. Go and never come back. You are not my daughter Nadezhda!

VALENTINA smiles triumphantly and makes a rude sign at NADEZHDA. She goes over to NIKOLAI and puts her arms around him.

NADEZHDA: Fine by me. Who wants you for a dad anyway? You're a mentally unstable, dirty old man. You cuddle up with your fat-bosom wife and leave me out of it.

NADEZHDA storms out. VALENTINA whoops.

VALENTINA: *(Calls out.)* And don't come back! Just because you are legal, you think you better than me!

NIKOLAI watches NADEZHDA go with sadness.

SCENE 10

VERA steps forward and reads out a letter.

VERA: To the Home Office Immigration department at Lunar House, Croydon.

Dear Sir/Madam,

Earlier this year Mrs Dubova obtained a second six months visa and arrived via Ramsgate in March. She once more moved into Mr Turner's house. She and my father were married at the Immaculate Conception in Peterborough in June.

After the wedding Mrs Dubova did not move in with our father, but carried on living at Hall Street in Mr Turner's house. When the term ended, Mrs Dubova (now Mayevskyj) and her son, Stanislav moved into our father's house. However, she did not share a room with our father and the marriage has never been consummated.

NADEZHDA steps forward too. She joins VERA and looks full of guilt. However she continues to read the letter.

NADEZHDA: At first things seemed to be working out all right. We believed that although Mrs Dubova (now Mayevskyj) might not love our father in a romantic sense, she would at least be kind and caring to a frail elderly man in his last years. However, after only a few months, things have begun to go very wrong.

Beat. NADEZHDA looks at VERA imploringly. VERA urges her on. NADEZHDA speaks with a shaky voice.

NADEZHDA: We, his daughters, fear for the safety of our father and urge you to consider deporting Mrs Dubova (now Mayevskyj) back to Ukraine.

> *NADEZHDA looks warily at VERA who in turn looks triumphant.*

SCENE 11

NIKOLAI is standing in his living room with a neatly dressed woman carrying notebook and pencil. A male assistant is with her.

BARBARA: My name is Barbara Michaels and I am the district Immigration Service Officer. This is my assistant Mr Emile.

MR EMILE: How d'you do.

> *They all shake hands. NIKOLAI is flustered.*

NIKOLAI: Very good. I am Nikolai Mayevskyj – although I was not expecting you.

BARBARA: We like to keep our visits under wraps so as to speak.

NIKOLAI: Like secret detectives?

BARBARA: Not quite, but as you can see, we need to confirm the legitimacy of your recent marriage to Valentina Maye.

NIKOLAI: Mayevskyj.

BARBARA: Right.

> *Mr EMILE is having a good look aroud the place.*

NIKOLAI: Very good, it is long overdue. As soon as Valentina's immigration status is confirmed, our love will be sealed forever.

BARBARA: Yes...

NIKOLAI: She is very young.

BARBARA: I had noted that.

NIKOLAI: But our love is strong. Look, I can show you my love poetry to her.

> *NIKOLAI runmages around desperately in some papers and produces scraps of paper. MR EMILE glances at them.*

MR EMILE: Looks like double Dutch to me.

NIKOLAI: Not Dutch – Ukrainian! Poor Valentina has been
so anxious and this has sometimes made her irritable, but
soon her troubles will be at an end.

MR EMILE: Troubles?

NIKOLAI: Her anxiety. Would you like some tea?

BARBARA: No, thank you.

NIKOLAI: Are you sure? No? What can I do to help you then?
Would you like to see more love poetry?

BARBARA: No – thank you.

NIKOLAI: Ah! I can show you our wedding photos. Now,
where did I put them?

> *NIKOLAI looks a little confused as he scrabbles around
> looking for photos.*

NIKOLAI: I had a professional photographer brought in
especially…

BARBARA: That won't be necessary Mr Majestic. I'm simply
here to assess your living circumstances so I can confirm
your marital status. Tell me, what are your sleeping
arrangements?

NIKOLAI: *(Confused.)* Arrangements?

MR EMILE: Where do you sleep?

NIKOLAI: I can show you upstairs. I have a room. Valentina
has a room and Stanislav, her son has a room. You see,
plenty room for everybody.

BARBARA: You sleep in a separate room from your wife?

NIKOLAI: It is a modern marriage. I may look old but I am a
very forward looking young man.

> *NIKOLAI giggles. BARBARA and MR EMILE exchange
> glances.*

BARBARA: *(Makes notes.)* I see.

NIKOLAI gestures to his table which is covered in a heap of untidy papers.

NIKOLAI: And this is my table. I prefer to eat by myself. Stanislav and Valentina eat in the kitchen. I cook for myself – look, Toshiba apples.

NIKOLAI produces a half eaten tray of his apple concoction from the microwave.

NIKOLAI: Cooked by Toshiba microwave. Full of vitamins. Would you like to try?

BARBARA and MR EMILE eye the Toshiba apples with thinly disguised disgust.

BARBARA: No. Thank you very much. And will I be able to meet Mrs... the Mrs?

NIKOLAI: She is at work.

BARBARA: When does she return from work?

NIKOLAI: She is always coming at different time. Sometimes early, sometimes late. Better you telephone first.

BARBARA: I see. Thank you. You have been most helpful.

BARBARA writes more in her notebook and then snaps it shut.

NIKOLAI: You want to come upstairs?

BARBARA: I've seen everything I need to make my report. I'll bid you good day.

BARBARA and MR EMILE exit. NIKOLAI looks pleased. He settles down in his chair and has a snooze. VALENTINA enters. She looks furious as she waves a letter in the air.

VALENTINA: Read this. What it say?

NIKOLAI wakes with a start. He takes the letter and reads it slowly, silently.

VALENTINA: Well?

NIKOLAI: It says...

VALENTINA: I know what it says. I know! My application to stay is refused. Why? Why?

NIKOLAI: *(Reads.)* 'The inspector has found no evidence of a genuine marriage.'

VALENTINA: You fault. This you fault!

NIKOLAI: I don't understand...they seemed so nice.

VALENTINA: You foolish idiot man. You giving all the wrong answer. Why you no show them you love-letter poem? Why you no show them wedding picture?

NIKOLAI: She did not ask to see a poem. She asked to see where we sleep.

VALENTINA: She see you no good man to go into woman bedroom.

NIKOLAI: You no good wife – shut husband out of bedroom.

VALENTINA: What you want in bedroom? Eh?

She spits at NIKOLAI.

VALENTINA: You flippy floppy, squishy-squashy!

VALENTINA puts her face right up to NIKOLAI's and starts to chant.

VALENTINA: Flippy floppy, squishy-squashy! Flippy floppy, squishy-squashy!

NIKOLAI: Stop! Stop!

VALENTINA: You inferior being – you insect to be squashed, imbecile to be locked away.

NIKOLAI: Stop it!

VALENTINA: You are dead corpse to be put in ground next to peasant wife!

NIKOLAI shoves VALENTINA away but she shoves him back so hard he falls badly and bangs his head.

NIKOLAI: Aaarghhh! Look what you've done?!

VALENTINA: Now you go crying to no-tits daughter. Help! Help! Nadia Verochka! Wife beating me! Ha! Ha! Husband should beat wife!

> *VALENTINA smiles at the sight of the collapsed and cowering NIKOLAI.*

Squishy-squashy.

NIKOLAI: Stop it!

VALENTINA: I appeal. I see a solicitor and I appeal against this decision. Tell them my husband mad.

NIKOLAI: Valenka...

VALENTINA: You are sick man. Sick in the head. Causing too much trouble. Too much crazy talking about tractors. Too much kiss-kiss. No good for eighty-four year man.

NIKOLAI: I am not sick. I am poet and engineer. By the way Valentina, you should remember that Nietzsche himself was considered to be mad by those who were his intellectual inferiors.

VALENTINA: I take you to doctor. I tell him about oralsex.

NIKOLAI: No Valya. Why must you talk about this to everybody?

VALENTINA: I will tell doctor – eighty-four-year-old husband want make oralsex. Squishy squashy husband want make oralsex.

> *NIKOLAI places his hands in anguish over his ears.*

VALENTINA: You useless shrivel-brain shrivel-penis donkey, You dried relic of ancient goat turd! Why you still living? You should be long ago lying beside Ludmilla, dead beside dead.

> *VALENTINA laughs cruelly at him and exits. NIKOLAI is left cowering on the floor. NADEZHDA enters and rushes towards him.*

NADEZHDA: Pappa! What are you doing down there?

NIKOLAI whimpers as NADEZHDA helps him up and sits him down in a chair.

She sees that his face is bleeding.

NADEZHDA: What happened?

NIKOLAI: Nadezhda. Good you came.

NADEZHDA: Pappa, what happened?

NIKOLAI: Not so good with Valentina. She is acting as if she rather dislikes me...

NADEZHDA: Did she hit you?

NIKOLAI: No. I fell.

NADEZHDA: She pushed you?

NIKOLAI nods.

NIKOLAI: She was denied immigrant status and she blames me.

NADEZHDA: I don't know what to say. Anybody could see this was going to happen.

NIKOLAI: Too bad. Whatever happens...at least until her appeal we will stay together...after that they will go and I will be left in peace.

NADEZHDA hugs NIKOLAI who cries a little.

Don't tell Vera will you?

NADEZHDA: Pappa!

NIKOLAI: She will laugh. You know what type Vera is.

NIKOLAI: Why are you always so angry with Vera? What did she do?

NIKOLAI: She was always autocrat, even when baby. Clinging to Ludmilla with fists of steel. Grip tight. Suck, suck, suck. Such a temper. Crying. Screaming.

NADEZHDA: She was only a baby. She couldn't help it.

NIKOLAI: Hmmm... And smoking all the time. Even around your mother's death bed. What a powerful tyrant is a cigarette. Did I ever tell you Nadia that I almost died from cigarettes?

NADEZHDA: Why do you always change the subject?

NIKOLAI: Because I didn't smoke, it almost cost me my life. You see, in that German labour camp at the end of the war, cigarettes were a currency followed by everybody.

NADEZHDA: You were in a German labour camp?

NIKOLAI: Me, your mother and Vera.

NADEZHDA: What?

NIKOLAI: Before you were born. When we worked, we got paid: so much bread, so much fat, so many cigarettes, we always had enough to eat, were always warm. That was how we survived through the war.

NADEZHDA: How is it that you never told me this before? Not even Mum?! How old was Vera?

NIKOLAI: Ten years old. Vera, unfortunately is now of course a smoker. Has she told you about her first encounter with cigarettes?

NADEZHDA: No, she didn't tell me anything. What do you mean? What happened with Vera and cigarettes?

NIKOLAI: Can't remember.

NADEZHDA: Pappa! Finish the story.

NIKOLAI: No point to remember.

NADEZHDA: You can remember. Tell me. It's important to me!

LUDMILLA enters with her suitcase and places it on the floor. She opens it and looks towards NIKOLAI. Light shines out of the suitcase and the ENSEMBLE enter expectantly – ready.

NADEZHDA: Pappa, please tell me.

All eyes are on NIKOLAI. But instead, he kicks the suitcase shut.

NIKOLAI: Too much in the past. It is the present I have to deal with now.

LUDMILLA, NADEZHDA and the ENSEMBLE look disappointed and exit.

ACT TWO

SCENE 1

LUDMILLA is sat with her suitcase under the cherry tree. She is busy mending a shirt with a needle and thread.

LUDMILLA: *(To the audience.)* Nikolai and I were class mates. He was always the first boy to put his hand up in class. I thought he was an insufferable know-it-all. But it was only when I rescued him from local bullies, that we got to know each other.

> *Ukrainian Music. Church bells.*

> *The ENSEMBLE are children now. A young NIKOLAI is walking along, huddled up from the cold and snow. He has a pair of ice skates slung around his neck. LUDMILA watches him as a snowball is lobbed at him. He turns to look at where it's coming from and he gets another snowball in his face.*

SOVINKO 1: Hey hey! Nikolashka! Clever-dick – who d'you fancy? Who d'you wank over?

> *Young NIKOLAI tries to walk away but the two bullies catch up with him.*

SOVINKO 2: Hey brain arse, d'yer fancy Ludmilla? Have you shown her your dick?

YOUNG NIKOLAI: I don't fancy anyone. I am interested languages and mathematics.

> *The SLOVINKO brothers laugh.*

SLOVINKO 1: Y'hear that? He don't fancy girls. Kick with the other foot do you?

> *YOUNG NIKOLAI looks confused.*

> *The two bullies chant.*

SLOVINKOS: *(Together.)* Gay boy! Gay boy! Likes it up the bum!

YOUNG NIKOLAI: Just because I don't fancy girls, it does not logically follow that I must fancy boys.

SLOVINKO 1: 'Logically'? You got a logical dick? C'mon then, let's see it.

YOUNG NIKOLAI: Leave me alone.

SLOVINKO 2: Let's cool his dick down a bit.

YOUNG NIKOLAI: No! No!

> *The two SLOVINKOs wrestle YOUNG NIKOLAI to the ground and pin him down. YOUNG NIKOLAI thrashes about as one of the SLOVINKO's starts to pull down his trousers as the other violently sits astride him.*

YOUNG NIKOLAI: *(Screams.)* Help me! Help me!

> *LUDMILLA, (now a young girl) steps forward, skates slung around her neck too.*
>
> *She pulls one of the SLOVINKOS off*

LUDMILLA: Get off him you big fat bully!

> *SLOVINKO 1 swats her away.*

SLOVINKO 1: Is he your boyfriend then? Fancy him do you?

> *LUDMILLA grabs SLOVINKO's hair in both hands and pulls it hard.*

LUDMILLA: You get off him right now or I'll call my Dad and he'll slice off your fingers with his sabre and stuff 'em up your nose!

> *The SLOVINKO's look afraid and stand up. They stand threateningly over LUDMILLA but she stands her ground. YOUNG NIKOLAI is pulling up his trousers and scrabbling to his feet.*

LUDMILLA: My dad knows where you live. Just behind the railways station – right? With your mum and little sisters. He'll pay you all a visit.

SLOVINKO 1: Mama!

> *He pulls his brother away and they run away.*

SLOVINKO 2: *(Calls back.)* Slag!

> *LUDMILLA looks at YOUNG NIKOLAI and puts her hand out to him.*

LUDMILLA: Are you okay?

YOUNG NIKOLAI: Yes. Thank you. I was going to the sports stadium to skate.

LUDMILA: Me too.

> *YOUNG NIKOLAI hesitantly takes LUDMILLA's hand. They both smile at each other. MUSIC as the two dance and skate. They twirl and spin and fall laughing into each other's arms.*

SCENE 2

A Rolls Royce car's bonnet can be now seen in one corner of the set. On the other side we can see a Rover bonnet.

Inside NIKOLAI's house:

VALENTINA's ornate and brightly coloured bras are all hanging on a washing line in the kitchen. VALENTINA is sat on a chair wearing a tight outfit, bare legs crossed with her peep toe sandals dangling off her feet. She is laughing and joking with a uniformed police officer, drinking tea. There is now a door which separates the kitchen from the lounge area.

The POLICEMAN looks at the bras in wonder.

VALENTINA: *(Waves at her bras.)* Excuse washing. Have to dry laundry – always raining here.

POLICEMAN: *(Delighted.)* No need to apologise.

VALENTINA: I work shifts – so little time for housework. Always I working – change beds, sheets, bed pans, these poor old people who – how you say – left to die by heartless relatives.

POLICEMAN: You've certainly got your work cut out for you. Don't think I could do it.

VALENTINA: They have stories these people. Always talking past. Fighting war against Nazis, dancing on stage, one man he make magic tricks for me.

POLICEMAN: Poor sods. Look where they've ended up.

VALENTINA: It is tragedy. In my country, we look after old. But not easy. My husband is old, is stubborn – like ox.

> *NADEZHDA enters and looks at the two. She stares at the bras in amazement. She introduces herself to the Police officer.*

NADEZHDA: Hello. I'm Nadezhda – Mr Mayevskyj's daughter.

VALENTINA: She call you. She tell you I am fighting with her father.

> *POLICEMAN stands up, trying to be more formal.*

POLICEMAN: Just dropped by to check on your dad.

NADEZHDA: Where is he?

VALENTINA: He lock himself in room. Refuse come out.

POLICEMAN: I did try.

> *NADEZHDA knocks on the door.*

NADEZHDA: Pappa, it's me, Nadia. You can unlock the door now. It's okay. I'm here. Please come out. Pappa? Pappa.

> *There is a rattle of a bolt being pulled back and NIKOLAI peeps round the door. NADEZHDA is shocked by his appearance. He looks emaciated, his long grey hair is straggly and messy. He has no trousers on.*

NADEZHDA: Pappa? Where are your trousers? Please put on your trousers. What's that smell?

VALENTINA: He shit himself.

> *The POLICEMAN looks at VALENTINA with a smirk.*

POLICEMAN: Blimey!

NADEZHDA: What happened Pappa?

NIKOLAI: She...she...

> *VALENTINA gives him a look.*

NADEZHDA: Tell me what happened?

NIKOLAI: She throw water at me.

VALENTINA: He was shout at me. Bad thing. Bad language speaking. I say shut up. He no shut up. I throw water. Is only water. Water no hurt.

POLICEMAN: Just a marital tiff. Looks like six of one and half a dozen of the other. Usually the case in domestics. Can't take sides.

NADEZHDA: Surely you can see what's going on?

POLICEMAN: As far as I'm aware, no crime has been committed. Happens all the time.

NADEZHDA: But isn't it your job to protect the vulnerable? Just look! Use your eyes! You can see there's a difference in size and strength – they're not exactly evenly matched are they?

POLICEMAN: *(Eyes VALENTINA lecherously.)* Can't arrest someone because of their size. 'Course I'll continue to keep an eye, if your dad would like me to.

NIKOLAI: You are no different to Stalin's police! Whole system of state apparatus is only to defend powerful against the weak.

POLICEMAN: Mr Mayevsky, we live in a free country and you are free to express your opinion. I better be off. Nice to have met you.

> *The POLICEMAN smiles at VALENTINA and exits.*
>
> *VALENTINA gets up and picks up her handbag.*

VALENTINA: You clean up you Pappa shit.

NADEZHDA: And I'll tidy up a bit too.

VALENTINA: I too much working, no time house working. Your father – he no give me money.

NADEZHDA: But he gives you half his pension.

VALENTINA: Pension no good. What can buy with pension?

NADEZHDA: Whose Rolls Royce is that on the drive?

VALENTINA: My new car. Is nice car.

NIKOLAI: Car is kaput.

VALENTINA: You mend car Mr engineer.

NIKOLAI: Rolls-Royce kaput. Lada kaput. Soon Rover kaput.
Only walking is not kaput. Ha! Ha!

VALENTINA: Soon you kaput.
I time go working now. Again.

   VALENTINA exits. NIKOLAI slumps in a chair.

NIKOLAI: I think she means to kill me.

NADEZHDA: Now you're being ridiculous.

NIKOLAI: You haven't heard the terrible things she says to me.
She said I will soon return where I belong – underground.
In Russian. Said all in Russian.

NADEZHDA: Pappa, the language doesn't matter.

NIKOLAI: No, on the contrary, language is supremely
important. In language are encapsulated not only thoughts
but cultural values...Russians are cold, heartless.

NADEZHDA: Please don't tell me you paid for that Rolls Royce?

NIKOLAI: Five hundred pounds. It's a four litre sedan sold to
her by Eric Pyke.

NADEZHDA: Who's Eric Pyke?

   ERIC PYKE enters.

NIKOLAI: Actually, he is most interesting type.

ERIC: Valentina's roller. Yes, it came from the Glaswyne estate.
It was used for many years as farm transportation – hay,
sheep, fertilizer bags...

NIKOLAI: Almost like tractor.

ERIC: I was was a pilot in the R.A.F. Jet propulsion fighter
pilot. Now I'm a used car dealer. And I have superb
moustaches.

   NADEZHDA turns to ERIC and addresses him.

NADEZHDA: How could you sell my father a car like that? You know the car doesn't even go.

ERIC: Well no, Miss er, Mrs er…Valentina said that her husband was a wizard engineer. Aeronautics. You see I happen to know a bit about planes. Some of the world leaders in aeronatics in the 1930s were Ukrainian. Sikorsky invented the helicopteer; Lozinsky worked…

NADEZHDA: But the Rolls Royce Mr Pyke?

ERIC: Valentina said her husband would get it going in no time. I had my doubts but she was very persuasive. You know what she's like.

NADEZHDA: *(Looks at ERIC.)* I know about you and Valentina Mr Pyke.

ERIC looks guilty and then at his watch.

ERIC: Is that the time? Must dash!

ERIC does a quick exit.

NADEZHDA: So, Pappa, you now have a Lada in the garage, a Rover on the drive and a Roller on the lawn?

NIKOLAI: None of the cars are licensed or insured. She wants me to repair the Roller. But my arthirits – I can't get under bonnet anymore.

NADEZHDA: This has gone too far Pappa. Listen, please. The good news is that she hasn't been granted leave to remain, which means she will be deported soon. But in the meantime, if you feel afraid of being in the house with her, you must come and stay with me and Mike.

NIKOLAI: If I leave the house, she will change the locks. I will be out, she will be in.

NADEZHDA: Pappa, you stink. Your room stinks. Clean yourself up and put some trousers on. I'm going to have a look around.

NADEZHDA notices, amongst the rotting apples a small machine/computer.

NADEZHDA: What is this? A Photocopier?

NIKOLAI: Valentina's new toy. She uses it to copy letters. Her letters. My letters.

NADEZHDA: She copies your letters? Where does she keep the copies?

NIKOLAI: Maybe in car. I see she takes everything to car.

NADEZHDA exits quickly.

NIKOLAI takes a bowl of water and starts to wash and tidy himself, putting on some fresh clothes, combing his hair etc. NADEZHDA re-enters with a large box bursting with papers. She scrabbles through them eagerly, quickly reading.

NADEZHDA: Your savings and pension accounts…bank statements… 'all this will be yours my beloved.'

NIKOLAI: Those I gave her. In the beginning.

NADEZHDA: Fool. …Who's in this photo?

NIKOLAI looks.

NIKOLAI: Her husband before me.

NADEZHDA: He actually looks quite decent.

And what's this Pappa?

NADEZHDA holds up a letter.

Feminine Beauty in Budapest? Receipt for payment of three thousand US Dollars in respect of breast enhancement surgery? Signed Dr Pavel Nagy?

NIKOLAI looks shifty as he sees the letter.

NIKOLAI: Hmmm…yes.

NADEZHDA: Three thousand dollars? Eighteen hundred pounds! You paid for Valentina's boob job? The money in the brown envelope!

NIKOLAI: Quite so.

NADEZHDA stares at her father in horror.

You are not talking to Vera about this.

NADEZHDA: You and Vera with your secrets. The only way you're going to be free again is if you divorce Valentina.

NIKOLAI: No.

NADEZHDA: She'll continue to abuse you.

NIKOLAI: You are like Vera. Did you know when Vera first discovered there was such a thing as divorce, she immediately tried to convince Ludmilla to divorce me? Now you try the same with Valentina.

NADEZHDA: Pappa, you lived with Mum for sixty years. Surely you can see that Valentina isn't the same as Mum?

NIKOLAI: Valentina is of quite different generation. She knows nothing of history, even less about recent past. She is daughter of Brezhnev era which is to bury all gone-by things and to become like in West. Always buying new things, new desires, something modern. It is not her fault; it is the post-war mentality.

NADEZHDA: But Pappa, she cannot abuse you like this!

NIKOLAI: One can forgive a beautiful woman many things.

NADEZHDA: For goodness' sake!

NIKOLAI: This Valentina, she is beautiful like Milla and like Milla she has strong spirit – but Milla was gentle. Did I ever tell you? First time I met Milla, I rescued her from local bullies? Valentina on the other hand has an element of cruelty in her nature unknown to Ludmilla, which by the way is characteristic of the Russian type.

NADEZHDA: How can you compare her to Mum? Vera's right, Mum should have divorced you years ago. You made her life a misery.

NIKOLAI: Misery? Nadia, why you always want to make a drama out of nothing?

NADEZHDA: You're the one who's always making drama. All my life, all Mum's life, we had to live with your craziness. Remember how upset Mum was when I was really little and you invited all those Ukrainians to come and live with us?

And what about when you left home and tried to catch the train back to Russia?

NIKOLAI: That was your fault! You were then a crazy Trotskyist.

NADEZHDA: I wasn't a Trotskyist.

NIKOLAI: I thought, why did I ever leave Russia? Why did I risk everything? Even my daughter was bringing communism here.

NADEZHDA: I went to Greenham Common to protest against the H bomb being deployed from there.

NIKOLAI: You were arrested and fined.

NADEZHDA: Three pounds. And even if I was a Trotskyist, I was only fifteen. You were an adult – supposedly.

NIKOLAI: All in the past Nadia. Why you have such bourgeois preoccupation with all personal history?

NADEZHDA: Because it's important Pappa.

NIKOLAI sits for a while in silence. He looks puzzled.

NIKOLAI: Millochka died. That is sad of course, but it is now in the past. Now is time for new life, new love.

NADEZHDA: I don't see any love here. You hiding in your room, soiling yourself, terrified.

NIKOLAI: I will not divorce.

NIKOLAI gets up and goes back into his room, locking it behind him.

SCENE 3

NADEZHDA is doing Tai Chi. Slow movements, deep breathing, obviously trying to calm herself. MIKE is sat by her rummaging through VALENTINA's box of papers.

MIKE: I can't believe that you stole all of these papers.

NADEZHDA: I didn't steal them. I copied the most important looking ones – just didn't have time to read them.

MIKE is intrigued as he goes through the copies.
NADEZHDA continues with her movements.

MIKE: It's all higgledy piggeldy – no order. Poems, letters in Ukrainian...receipts...

NADEZHDA: You should see her bedroom. An absolute mess.

MIKE: Nadia – you snoop!

NADEZHDA: I want to know what she's up to.

MIKE: Marriage certificate...here's a letter from Valentina's solicitor...

NADEZHDA: What does it say?

MIKE: Advises her to apply for legal aid...the tribunal hearing for her immigration status appeal is in September. The solicitor says: 'You are advised that you should avoid at all costs giving your husband grounds for divorce, as this could seriously jeopardise your case...'

NADEZHDA: The hearing's in September? That's months away.

MIKE peers at another letter.

MIKE: What's this?

NADEZHDA: What?

MIKE: It's dated 1961. Seems to be a report from a psychiatrist at the infirmary on your father.

NADEZHDA: Psychiatrist's report? I was right then! He's mad!

MIKE quickly reads it.

ENSEMBLE: A psychiatrist in a white coat steps forward

NADEZHDA: Well? What does it say?

MIKE: It doesn't matter.

NADEZHDA: What?

MIKE: It's nothing...

PSYCHIATRIST: Mr Mayevskj requested to see a psychiatrist because he believed he was suffering from a pathological hatred of his daughter.

NADEZHDA: Vera!

PSYCHIATRIST: I talked to Mr Mayevskj at length and
concluded that in view of his experience of communism it
was not at all surprising, natural in fact, that he should hate
his daughter for her communist views.

NADEZHDA: But Vera's not communist – never has been.

NADEZHDA realizes.

Wait. ...Oh – My – God. Was he talking about me?

MIKE: Your brush with Trotskyism.

*NADEZHDA snatches the report from MIKE and reads
it with horror.*

PSYCHIATRIST: So obsessive and all consuming was his hatred
of his younger daughter, that Mr Mayevskj feared it was a
sign of mental illness.

NADEZHDA looks enraged.

NADEZHDA: So he hates me as well as Vera?

MIKE: He clearly struggled – but he obviously got over it – all
in the past Nadezhda – don't get upset.

NADEZHDA bursts into tears. She starts to sob.

NADEZHDA: It was Mum's family who suffered unspeakable
wrongs – she had far more reason for hating me for being a
communist. She never stopped loving me even when I was
a wild teenager. I said horrid things to her... but she loved
me...how could Pappa? How dare he!

*MIKE stands and wraps his arms around NADEZHDA
to try and comfort her.*

MIKE: Nadezhda – he knew he was irrational and wrong,
which is why he asked to see a shrink.

NADEZHDA continues to sob.

MIKE: The real question is how did Valentina get hold of this?
And why is she holding on to it?

NADEZHDA: To prove what we all know – that he's mentally ill!

MIKE: Eccentric – Nadezhda.

> *The phone rings. Both MIKE and NADEZHDA look at the phone. MIKE picks up the phone and answers it.*

MIKE: Hullo? Yes…okay…I'll tell her.

> *MIKE puts down the phone and looks at NADEZHDA with pity.*

MIKE: I'm sorry love, but it's back to battle stations again. Vera will meet you at your father's.

SCENE 4

We hear NADEZHDA's voice shouting.

NADEZHDA: How dare you! You're taking advantage of an old man!

> *The neighbour – a retired businessman enters walking backwards onto the stage, chased by a furious NADEZHDA.*

NADEZHDA: Three thousand measly pounds? You knew my mother – you saw how much she loved that garden!

NEIGHBOUR: I was only trying to be helpful. Your father said he was having financial difficulties and needed to liquidate his assets.

NADEZHDA: Of course he's having financial difficulties with that blood sucking wife of his! You should be keeping an eye on him not encouraging him. What kind of a neighbour are you? Preying on the vulnerable elderly.

> *The neighbour looks terrified of NADEZHDA.*

NEIGHBOUR: Of course I won't buy the land. It was all a misunderstanding.

NADEZHDA: So you didn't offer to buy it?

NEIGHBOUR: I did…but I won't…of course if you and your sister…don't want to interfere…

NADEZHDA: Good.

NEIGHBOUR: She doesn't seem a very nice sort of lady, if you don't mind me saying. She sunbathes in the garden wearing…wearing…well not wearing…and I think she's having an affair. I've seen a man…hoots his car horn and out she comes running, all dressed up to the nines. All fur coat and no knickers, as my mother used to say.

NADEZHDA: Thank you for telling me. That's very useful information.

> *The NEIGHBOUR exits hurriedly. VALENTINA enters, arms folded, looking furious.*

VALENTINA: Why you go for next-door, nose pock?

> *NADEZHDA pushes past her and enters the house. NIKOLAI enters, following closely behind*

NADEZHDA: I've spoken to the people next door Pappa. They are no longer interested in buying Mum's garden.

NIKOLAI: Nadezhda! Why can't you leave me alone?

NADEZHDA: Because if I leave you alone, Pappa, this vulture will peck out your liver.

NIKOLAI: Eagle, eagle.

NADEZHDA: What eagle?

NIKOLAI: Eagle pecked out liver of Prometheus because he has brought fire.

NADEZHDA: You are not Prometheus, you are a pitiful, confused and deluded old man, who through your own idiocy have fallen prey to this she wolf…

> *VALENTINA lets out a howl of fury as she shoves NADEZHDA hard in the chest.*
>
> *NADEZHDA staggers back.*

NADEZHDA: How dare you!

> *NIKOLAI tries to protect NADEZHDA but VALENTINA pushes him too.*

NIKOLAI: Valya, Valya! Please no violence.

VALENTINA: You dog-eaten-brain-old-bent-stick, you go room, you shut up.

> *VALENTINA produces a key from her pocket and dangles it in front of NIKOLAI's nose.*

VALENTINA: I have room key! Ha! Ha! I have key room

> *NIKOLAI makes a grab for the key, but she holds it just above his reach. NIKOLAI makes a pathetic little jump.*

NIKOLAI: Valya, please give key!

> *VERA enters the fray and pulls out a Dictaphone from her bag and holds it up.*

VERA: I have a microphone! I will get evidence of your criminal activity! Now please Valentina, give my father back the key to his room and try to behave in a calm and civilized manner.

> *VALENTINA looks shocked.*

VALENTINA: Who you are?

VERA: How do you do. My name is Vera.

NADEZHDA: Hullo Vera! You've lost some weight.

VERA: Thank you. I'm on a new regime.

NIKOLAI: No Vera! I ask you not to come.

VERA: I had to come Pappa to sort out your mess. Such a fool Pappa. How could you marry such an awful woman?

> *VERA tries to grab the key off VALENTINA but the two end up fighting instead, rolling around on the floor, they get into a real cat fight. NIKOLAI seizes the moment and snatches the key from VALENTINA's grasp. VALENTINA jumps up and with her stilletoed heels kicks both VERA and NIKOLAI. She grabs the key and shoves NIKOLAI into his room and locks the door. She is triumphant as VERA rolls around on the floor in agony. NADEZHDA tries to help VERA.*

NADEZHDA: Oh my God Vera. Are you okay?

VERA: I have it all on tape! Everything you say is on tape!

VALENTINA: Good! This is what I want say you bitch vixen no-tits, you jealous.

> *VALENTINA shoves her hands under her breasts and*
> *makes little pouting kisses with her mouth.*

I know Vera, you no have man. I have plenty man. You dried up lonely old she-cat. Man like tits. You Pappa like tits. No man, not even you Pappa like you.

> *There is a knock on the door. A MAN enters carrying a*
> *big envelope.*

MAN: Mrs Mayevsky?

VALENTINA: Yes?

MAN: For you.

VALENTINA: Thank you

> *The MAN hands over the envelope.*

MAN: Divorce papers.

VALENTINA: Divorce pepper? I no want divorce.

MAN: No. The petitioner is Mr Nikolai Mayevski. He is divorcing *you.*

> *The MAN exits.*

VALENTINA: *(Shrieks)* Nikolai! Nikolai! What this is?

> *NIKOLAI is laughing loudly on the other side of the door.*

VALENTINA: *(To VERA.)* This you. Flesh eating she-cat-witch. You do this!

NADEZHDA: Actually, it was Pappa.

VERA: I'm sorry Valentina, but this is no more than you deserve. You cannot come to this country and deceive and cheat people, however stupid they are.

VALENTINA: I no cheat! You cheat! I love you Pappa! I love!

VERA: Don't be silly Valentina. Now go and see your solicitor.

> *VALENTINA starts to sob.*

VALENTINA: *(Upset.)* You want send me back? My son? My Stanislav! What happen to him? What will be his future? How can you do this to a woman from your country? You and sister, you monster!

VERA: Not only do we want to send you back, but we want you out of our mother's house.

SCENE 5

LUDMILLA's GRAVE.

LUDMILLA is tending the grave under the cherry tree. She is digging with a trowel and planting flowers.

LUDMILLA: *(To the audience.)* Nikolai's family disapproved of my family. They thought I was pretty enough but too wild and it was unfortunate that my Pappa was an 'enemy of the people'. My mother in turn thought Nikolai's family were pretentious and peculiar.

But Nikolai and I didn't care. We were in love.

LUDMILLA stands and smooths down her dress and the YOUNG NIKOLAI steps forward as Wedding music plays. They both kneel together in front of a COMMUNIST PARTY OFFICIAL as she reads the wedding vows in Ukrainian.

LUDMILLA: We were married at the registry office in Luhansk in 1936. There were no golden domes or bells and no one cried.

LUDMILLA and YOUNG NIKOLAI kiss. We hear the piercing cry of a baby. LUDMILLA sits on the bench, rocking the baby as it screams.

ENSEMBLE:

AUNT SHURA enters. Red hair, rolling a cigarette.

LUDMILLA: My Aunty Shura was a doctor and she delivered my first baby, Verochka. She was born in Luhansk in March 1937. Her crying drove Nikolai to distraction. Aunty Shura loved me but didn't think much of him.

YOUNG NIKOLAI paces in anguish as the baby cries. LUDMILA rocks the baby and desperately tries to quieten her. AUNT SHURA smokes her ciggy and watches YOUNG NIKOLAI with obvious dislike.

LUDMILLA: Shh...shhhh...

YOUNG NIKOLAI: I can't think! I can't read or write! Always screaming, screaming!

AUNT SHURA: Do us all a favour then, get out of the house and get a job.

YOUNG NIKOLAI: If I could get a job, I would! There's nothing suitable for me in Luhansk.

LUDMILLA: Stop shouting, you're upsetting the baby.

YOUNG NIKOLAI: Everything upsets that baby.

AUNT SHURA: You upset the baby.

YOUNG NIKOLAI: It's getting on my nerves.

LUDMILLA: You're getting on my nerves.

AUNT SHURA: Good for nothing.

> *AUNT SHURA and NIKOLAI have a blazing row.*
> *LUDMILLA sits with her baby, looking upset.*

AUNT SHURA: You are a selfish, useless man.

YOUNG NIKOLAI: Why are you always picking on me?

AUNT SHURA: You bring nothing to the table, nothing to the house. Awkward, stupid man. It's only because I love Ludmilla, that you have a roof over your head.

YOUNG NIKOLAI: I don't want to be here. You people, always making trouble, always criticising…

LUDMILLA: Tempers, shouting, oh! The door slamming. It was cramped, no hot water and sometimes there was no cold water. No famine but still, not enough food. Vera, poor Vera, she sucked ferociously at my breast but I was sick and anaemic. Not enough milk to give her.

> *AUNT SHURA takes out an apple from her pocket and hands it to LUDMILLA.*

AUNT SHURA: Take this apple, push iron nails into it, leave it overnight, then take the nails out and eat it – that way you get both vitamin C and iron.

YOUNG NIKOLAI picks up a bag, puts on his hat and kisses LUDMILLA briefly. He leaves without saying 'goodbye' to AUNTY SHURA.

LUDMILLA: Nikolai returned to Kiev to work at the Red Plough. His first design as an engineer was to make a concrete mixer. Very proud of that he was.

AUNTY SHURA gives LUDMILLA a letter. LUDMILLA tears it open excitedly.

LUDMILLA: *(To AUNTY SHURA.)* I got a place at the veterinary college in Kiev! Impossible! How can I go?

AUNTY SHURA: You must go. I'll look after Verochka.

LUDMILLA reluctantly hands over her screaming baby to AUNTY SHURA.

LUDMILLA: I left Verochka with my aunt Shura to go to college and to live with my husband. My aunt bought me a new coat and a hat.

AUNT SHURA hands over a hat and a coat. LUDMILLA puts on the hat with the veil.

LUDMILLA: Poor Vera. She clung to me, crying. They had to hold her back while I boarded the train.

LUDMILLA takes off her hat and looks sad.

LUDMILLA: I did not see Vera for two years and when I went back to fetch her at the start of the war, she didn't recognize me. I was thin and dishevelled. She shouted 'She's not my mother. My mother wears a hat!'

LUDMILLA looks proudly at the newly planted flowers.

SCENE 6

VALENTINA steps forward. She is now dressed somberly in smart, formal clothes. She is even wearing a hat, not dissimilar to LUDMILLA's NIKOLAI enters also dressed smartly in a suit. They both look up as if addressing a Judge before them in the audience.

NIKOLAI: Yes, I wish to apply for an injunction against my wife of just one year – she has been violent to me. I want her to leave my house on the basis that I am not safe in her company.

VALENTINA: I love husband. He mistaken.

NIKOLAI: There were witnesses at the hospital. She pushed me down the steps, in a public place and I cut my forehead.

VALENTINA: This not true!

NIKOLAI: Her personality is aggressive and violent towards me. She locked me in my bedroom.

VALENTINA: I am not bad woman. He has a paranoia!

NIKOLAI: In one incident, yes, she attacked both my older daughter Vera and myself with her stiletto heels.

VALENTINA: This untruth. He is very imagination man.

NIKOLAI: There are sworn statements from a nurse at the hospital, from where she was ejected for aggressive behaviour.

VALENTINA: This is lie. He mad, making stories.

NIKOLAI: It is not a lie. You can see from my psychiatrist report that I am sound of mind. And she is also adulteress.

VALENTINA: No! I faithful to husband.

NIKOLAI: I have evidence to prove she is seeing another man – Eric Pyke. Is a note from him. Signed.

VALENTINA: Please, please, I beg. I nowhere else to live with son.

NIKOLAI lifts a shaky hand and points it at VALENTINA.

NIKOLAI: I believe she wishes to murder me!

VALENTINA turns and looks at NIKOLAI, disbelieving and puzzled.

SCENE 7

NIKOLAI's HOUSE.

NADEZHDA, MIKE and NIKOLAI crack open a bottle of purple plum wine. They are elated as they all laugh and shout 'cheers'!

NIKOLAI rummages around in his papers and finds the page he is looking for. As he produces it, the ENSEMBLE enters and joins in as before.

POEM 3

NIKOLAI: *This century grew dark and history records*
How we turned our ploughshares into swords
Ukraine's Kharkiv Locomotive Factory
Was converted to ends less satisfactory
Turning out tanks for the fields of battle
Slaughtering people like so much cattle.

The T34 with caterpillar tracks
Had armoured plating to the max
Paraded in Moscow and much adored
It's credited with turning the tide of the war.
But the tank with the most ferocious design –
A true killing machine – was the Valentine.

Exiled Ukrainians helped the construction
Of this British and Canadian production:
The Valentine tank, a machine of hate
Born Valentine's day 1938
Clumsy, old-fashioned, unlovely, heavy,
Without compassion, ugly and deadly.

> *NIKOLAI holds up a small plug which he hands over to MIKE.*

MIKE: What's this?

NIKOLAI: I find it plugged in my room, under my bed.

NADEZHDA: A baby alarm?

NIKOLAI: The other one's plugged in upstairs in her room. She was listening to everything. My phone calls to you! To Solicitor – like evil Stasi. Spy.

MIKE: That's quite clever.

NIKOLAI: Do you know the theory of panopticon? English philosopher Jeremy Bentham. Is designed for the perfect prison. Jailer sees everything, from every angle and yet himself remains invisible. So Valentina knows everything about me and I know nothing about her.

NADEZHDA: Outrageous!

MIKE: But I still feel uncomfortable about her being deported. It's a cruel way to deal with Valentina.

NADEZHDA: Hmmm...yes...but...

MIKE: She came for a better life. For her son. Things are bad in Ukraine.

NADEZHDA: Mike – she gave us no choice.

They all fall silent when they see VALENTINA standing in the doorway carrying bags. STANISLAV struggles past heaving an enormous suitcase. He does not say anything. VALENTINA gives everyone a hard stare.

MIKE: Can I help you carry those?

VALENTINA: I no want help.

VALENTINA walks past with as much dignity as she can muster. They all watch her as she turns one last time.

VALENTINA: You think you very clever, Mr Engineer, but you wait. Remember I always get what I want.

She leaves and slams the door behind her. NIKOLAI looks crushed.

NADEZHDA hugs NIKOLAI.

NADEZHDA: Pappa – You alright?

NIKOLAI: All right. Yes everything all right. Good job. Maybe one day I will telephone Valentina and seek reconciliation.

ACT THREE

SCENE 1

SIX MONTHS LATER.

MIKE and NIKOLAI are looking at a man (DUBOV) who has just entered the lounge. He steps forward and extends his hand to MIKE.

MAN: I am Dubov.

MIKE: *(Mystified.)* Dubov?

NIKOLAI: Ah! Dubov! Highly esteemed Director of Polytechnic in Ternopil! Renowned leading Ukrainian scholar! You are most welcome in my modest house.

MIKE: Hold on – Dubov? Isn't that…?

NIKOLAI: Yes! Valentina's intelligent type husband.

DUBOV: Mayevskyj! Acclaimed engineer of first order! I have been honoured to read your fascinating thesis on tractor history which you sent to me.

NIKOLAI: And this is my son-in-law Mikhail Lewis

MIKE: *(Shakes hands.)* How do you do.

NIKOLAI: Distinguished trade unionist and computer expert.

DUBOV: Very happy to meet you.

> *DUBOV grabs MIKE and gives him two manly kisses on the cheek. MIKE is rather taken aback.*

NIKOLAI: Sit, sit down. We are having some of my wife's – my late wife's – excellent four year old plum wine.

MIKE: Let me pour you some.

DUBOV: *Dyakuyu*, I would like.

> *MIKE gets busy pouring some wine for everyone. DUBOV raises his glass.*

DUBOV: Nazdarovya!

NIKOLAI & MIKE: Nazdarovya!

DUBOV downs his drink in one. MIKE pours him another.

NIKOLAI: Why are you here Dubov?

DUBOV: I have come to find my wife and son. I have letters, letters – Stanislav is unhappy at school where he says boys lazy, obsessed with sex and academic standard is low. Valentina – also writes she unhappy. Say new husband is violent, paranoid man.

MIKE: That's you Nikolai.

DUBOV: But now I meet respected gentleman-engineer I think maybe she exaggerate?

NIKOLAI: Ah women.

DUBOV: She is sometimes known to exaggerate.

MIKE: Just a little.

DUBOV: One may forgive a beautiful woman a little exaggeration. The important thing is that now is time for her to come home.

MIKE: But aren't you divorced?

DUBOV: I have over to England on exchange programme with Leicester University to extend my knowledge of super conductivity and I have some leave now. My mission. Find Valentina! Win her and win back her heart. She loved me once. She can love me again.

MIKE and NIKOLAI are silent, slightly stunned.

DUBOV: I am coming here on train from Leicester, looking, looking – but where is she? Where is Stanislav?

MIKE: They don't live here anymore.

DUBOV: No?

MIKE: We don't know where they are.

NIKOLAI: Six months – gone Dubov. She has even left two cars here.

DUBOV: Rolls Royce?

NIKOLAI: Yes. But is kaput.

DUBOV: But she cannot be far – no?

MIKE: To be honest Dubov, no one has seen her.

DUBOV: But you will help me find her? She must come back.

NIKOLAI: This you must discuss with Valentina – if you can find her. My impression is she is absolutely determined she must stay in Britain.

DUBOV: She is afraid of being sent back to Ukraina.

MIKE: But is Ukraina so frightening?

DUBOV: At this time – yes. Our beloved mother-country is in the grip of criminals and gangsters.

MIKE: It's all that neo liberal bollocks. The crooks grab all the wealth, consolidate it into so-called legitimate businesses. Rockefeller, Carnegie, Morgan – they all started off as robber barons. Now the sun shines out of their million dollar foundations.

NIKOLAI: Once the fabric of civil society is torn apart, they flourish like weeds in a newly ploughed field.

DUBOV: Once we were a nation of farmers and engineers. We were not rich, but we had enough. Now racketeers prey on our industries, while our educated youth fly westwards in search of wealth. Our national export is the sale of beautiful young women into prostitution to feed the monstrous appetites of the Western male. It is a tragedy.

MIKE is all fired up.

MIKE: Yes – a tragedy!

DUBOV: They laugh at us. They suppose such corruption is in our nature but I would argue that it is merely characteristic of the type of economy which has been thrust upon us.

NIKOLAI: Well said Dubov!

DUBOV: Yes, for such a beautiful flower as Valentina, the wind of Ukrainia blows very hard and cold at this moment. But it will not always be so. And where there is love, there is always enough warmth for the human soul to thrive.

NIKOLAI: Big snag Dubov. She hates me. Does not want to be found.

MIKE: I'm sure we can help Nikolai. Nadezhda might know where to start looking. How long do you have before you have to return?

DUBOV: Only three weeks. I have come so far. To leave without seeing my Valentina!

DUBOV starts to weep. NIKOLAI puts his arm around DUBOV's shoulder.

NIKOLAI: Come, come Volodya Simenovich, be a man.

DUBOV: Alas, Nikolai Alexeevich, to be a man is to be a weak and fallible creature.

NIKOLAI: You must come and stay here with me. You can have Valentina's old room. You will be comfortable here. We can talk about engineering – yes? And I can make you my special dish – Toshiba apples.

DUBOV: Thank you. You are most kind.

MIKE stands and raises a glass of the plum wine.

MIKE: Cheer up everybody. Raise your glasses.

MIKE looks at the odd couple before him. He thinks.

MIKE: To the triumph of the human spirit!

DUBOV and NIKOLAI raise their glasses and then drink.

DUBOV & NIKOLAI: Nazdarovya!

SCENE 2

NADEZHDA and VERA are sat together in a café drinking tea. LUDMILLA sits between them. She is cutting and peeling vegetables.

Whilst they are talking, we see DUBOV exit and re-enter with a small rucksack with all his clothes neatly folded inside. He starts to take them out whilst NIKOLAI gets busy making his Toshiba apples.

VERA: The triumph of the human spirit! That is charming but quite naive. Let me tell you, the human spirit is mean and selfish; the only impulse is to preserve itself. Everything else is pure sentimentality.

NADEZHDA: That's what you always say Vera. But what if the human spirit is noble and generous – creative, empathic, imaginative, spiritual – and sometimes it's just not strong enough to withstand all the meanness and selfishness of the world?

VERA: Spiritual? Really Nadia. Where do you think all the meanness and selfishness come from, if not the human spirit? I know what people are like deep down.

NADEZHDA: And I don't?

VERA: Some things it is better not to know.

NADEZHDA: You're wearing Mum's locket.

VERA: She gave it to me.

NADEZHDA: You took the locket.

VERA: Nadezhda, please don't start.

NEDEZHDA: You pressurized Mum into signing the codicil. Split the money equally among three granddaughters, instead of two daughters. That way you and yours get yours twice as much. Greedy.

VERA: *(Aghast.)* Is this why you stopped all contact with me for two whole years? It wasn't exactly a fortune.

NADEZHDA: It's the principle of the matter. I want things to be fair. The money, the locket – you went behind my back and put pressure on Mum when she was dying.

VERA: You weren't there, were you? You were off pursuing your career – leaving all the responsibility to me. As always.

NADEZHDA: I was working! You tormented Mum's last days with stories of your divorce, of your husband's cruelty. You chain smoked at her bedside whilst she lay dying.

VERA: Stop whining.

NADEZHDA: Mum loved us both equally. She wanted us to share what she left behind.

VERA: She could only give the locket to one of us. She gave it to me because I was there when she needed me.

NADEZHDA: You barged in and took over.

VERA: I had to – because you ran away. Couldn't face Mum's illness, her terrible final days, could you?

NADEZHDA: I work for a living. You never did a day's work in your life. You always had Big Dick with his expense account, his share options, his annual bonuses, his clever little deals and dodgy ways of avoiding tax. Then when it all went wrong, you tried to fleece him for every penny he had. Mum always said she could understand why he divorced you. You were so nasty to him. Your own mother said that Vera!

VERA: It's easy to be superior when you don't know what hardship is. When you're in a trap, you have to fight your way out.

NADEZHDA falls silent.

LUDMILLA: Vera and Nadia – When me and your Pappa are gone – you will just have each other. You will have to stop fighting and learn to set your differences aside. It is important. You are family.

NADEZHDA: Why are you so bitter Vera?

VERA: I'm bitter?

VERA looks away – silent. Beat.

NADEZHDA: Anyway, Valentina's disappeared. I don't know where she's gone. But Pappa and Dubov seem to be getting on like a house on fire. He cooks, he cleans, he listens to pappa yakking on about his tractor history.

VERA: Dubov could be the perfect wife.

VERA and NADEZHDA laugh heartily.

DUBOV is offered the Toshiba apples by NIKOLAI. He eats and relishes it.

DUBOV: That is most delicious thing I ever tasted in my life!

NIKOLAI claps his hands in glee. DUBOV exits and re enters with an assortment of car parts which he lays out on the floor. MIKE re-enters carrying a six pack. He stands and studies the car parts on the floor with DUBOV and NIKOLAI as he doles out the beer.

NADEZHDA: I went to see Eric Pyke.

ERIC PYKE with his moustaches steps forward.

ERIC PYKE: *(Upset.)* I haven't seen Valentina for months. I know she was uspet with your father – but I didn't do anything wrong! I miss her. If you see her, tell her...tell her...I miss her!

NADEZHDA: There was another chap after him... Bald Ed.

A BALD MAN steps forward.

ED: *(Upset.)* Valentina was staying with me and then she left. Just vanished. Don't know where she went or how to find her.

VERA: She gets about.

ED: I even went to the Ukrainian club but no one's seen her there either. If you see her, tell her...tell her ...I miss her!

VERA: What about the first chap she stayed with – Bob?

A bare chested ENSEMBLE steps forward with a placard which simply reads in big letters:

BOB TURNER HAS EMIGRATED TO AUSTRALIA WITH HIS WIFE.

NADEZHDA: All I could do was leave messages everywhere – telling Valentina her husband – her first husband has come looking for her and Stanislav.

DUBOV: Mikhael, I have diagnosis for Rolls Royce sickness.

MIKE: Really?

DUBOV: She is leaking oil because the plug is loose. As for the suspension sag, the most likely problem is a broken spring bracket and the reason she does not run is probably an electrical fault, maybe the generator or the alternator.

NIKOLAI: First class engineer!

MIKE: Do you think you can fix it?

DUBOV: With the right parts.

NIKOLAI: We don't have key. Valentina has it.

DUBOV: We make new ignition.

NADEZHDA: And now all the men are obsessing with fixing the Roller. Mike's been searching scrap dealers and finding spare parts. They all spend time poring over technical manuals that Mike's downloaded from the internet.

VERA: How ludicrous! Men – a total mystery aren't they?

NADEZHDA: There I must agree with you.

SCENE 3

VALENTINA enters and stands FOS. She is heavily pregnant. She hesitates before entering NIKOLAI's lounge. No one is there. She looks anxious.

VALENTINA: Ello! Ello! Volodya!

> *NADEZHDA enters and gasps when she sees VALENTINA's belly.*

NADEZHDA: Hi Valentina. Glad you could make it. I see you must have got my messages.

> *VALENTINA sneers at NADEZHDA and pushes past her calling for DUBOV*

VALENTINA: Ello! Ello! Volodya!

NADEZHDA: He is here, but he's gone out.

VALENTINA: Is nobody here. You tell me lying.

NADEZHDA: Look, his bag is here.

> *VALENTINA picks up the green rucksack and sits heavily clutching it to her.*
>
> *She seems lost in thought.*

NADEZHDA: When's your baby due?

> *VALENTINA doesn't respond.*

NADEZHDA: Is Ed the father? Ed at the Imperial hotel?

VALENTINA: Why you go nose pock in every place? Eh?

NADEZHDA: He seems a very nice man.

VALENTINA: Is nice man. Is no bebby father.

> *VALENTINA sits quietly thoughtful, for once, not raging. NADEZHDA sits quietly beside her.*
>
> *They hear the sound of men's voices as MIKE, NIKOLAI and DUBOV enter.*
>
> *They all stand stock still when they see VALENTINA sat there. DUBOV rushes over to hug VALENTINA but then stops when he sees VALENTINA's pregnant state.*

DUBOV: I have been searching and searching for you my darling.

VALENTINA: Too late. You come too late.

> *STANISLAV runs in and collides into DUBOV's arms. The two have a joyful reunion.*

DUBOV: My boy! My son! How you have grown! Let me look at you.

STANISLAV: Pappa! Pappa! You're here! I can't believe it.

DUBOV: I am here to take you and your mother home.

STANISLAV: Pappa – why did you take so long to come?

DUBOV: I'm sorry…I'm here now.

> *STANISLAV sits with DUBOV on the sofa and hugs his son close to him.*

NIKOLAI: You are big with baby Valentina. Who is the father?

VALENTINA: You are bebby father.

NIKOLAI: *(Squeaks.)* Me?

> *NIKOLAI looks delightedly at NADEZHDA and MIKE.*

NADEZHDA: Hang on a minute Valentina. You can't get pregnant from oral sex you know.

VALENTINA: Why you know oralsex?

NIKOLAI: Nadia! Please!

DUBOV: Valenka darling. Maybe when you were in Ukraina last time...? I know it is a long time...

VALENTINA: Eighteen months.

DUBOV: ...but where there is love, all miracles are possible. Maybe this baby has been waiting for our reunion to bless us.

VALENTINA: Not possible. I am still married to Nikolai. I am still Mrs Mayevskyj and I am carrying husband bebby.

> *VALENTINA stands. Holding the father's eyes, she slides her hands around her breasts and down over her belly. NIKOLAI quivers.*

DUBOV: Kolya, don't be a fool.

NIKOLAI: You are the fool. Whoever heard of a baby carried for eighteen months? Only happens with elephants. Valentina is not an elephant.

NADEZHDA: Pappa, you can't conceive a child by oral sex or through some kind of platonic exchange of minds.

> *MIKE laughs out loud but stops when everyone stares him out.*

DUBOV: It matters not who fathered the child, but who will be the father to it.

VALENTINA: You no bebby father.

NIKOLAI: You no bebby father Dubov! I bebby father!

> *VERA enters.*

VERA: There is only one answer. The baby must have a paternity test. If there is a baby at all. I bet it's just a pillow pushed up inside her jumper.

> *VALENTINA screams with terror when VERA lunges forward to try and feel VALENTINA's belly.*

VALENTINA: No! No! You cholera-sick-eat-bebby witch! You no put hand on me!

> *DUBOV tries to go forward to hug VALENTINA but she pushes him off and walks away.*

VALENTINA: If you want divorce Nikolai, you have to pay me £20,000. Then only I go.

NIKOLAI: Maybe I won't divorce you.

DUBOV: Nikolai Alexeevich, Vera and Nadia had the benefit of your parental wisdom when they were growing. Stanislav also needs to be with his father. As for the baby – a young child needs a young father. Be content with those children you already have.

NIKOLAI: You're not so young yourself Volodya Simenovich

DUBOV: Indeed not. But I am much younger than you.

VALENTINA: Twenty thousand pounds Nikolai. For bebby.

NIKOLAI: I won't give you a divorce.

VALENTINA: I'll see you in court.

VERA: And we'll make sure the courts don't grant you a penny! You've already screwed enough out of Pappa.

STANISLAV jumps up furious.

STANISLAV: Enough! NO MORE!

Everyone stops and stares at him as STANISLAV erupts.

You're supposed to be grown ups, but you behave like imbecile, selfish children. All of you are as bad as each other. I want to be with my Pappa. Mama, you want to be with Pappa – so let's stop all this nonsense. Nikolai is too ancient to be a father and I am sick of all your constant fighting. You are shit parents – all of you! What kind of an example are you to me? I want to run away from all of you and tear my skin off. I'm sick to death of you all.

VALENTINA is shocked as STANISLAV starts to cry. She gathers him to her.

VALENTINA: My *holubchik*. I am sorry…don't cry…all is for you…everything I do…

DUBOV stands and hugs STANISLAV too.

DUBOV: All will be fine…don't cry my son. Shhh…don't upset yourself. You are right. We are all imbeciles.

NIKOLAI: I am not imbecile. I am poet-engineer.

VERA: Be quiet Pappa.

NIKOLAI: But...

NADEZHDA: Yeah, shut up Pappa.

*We end with VALENTINA , DUBOV and STANISLAV all
hugging each other and everyone else watching them.*

SCENE 4

POEM 4

NIKOLAI: *With the end of the war we can now espouse
How finally swords were turned into ploughs;
The world needed feeding and a crucial factor
Would be technical advances with the tractor.
An American name now rises up clear
A Vermont blacksmith called John Deere.*

*In the 1830s his plough was primary
In opening up the wild-west prairie
So John Deere's company grew at a pace
To become one of the biggest in the States.
In the post-war years Deere's name gained prominence
Illustrating American dominance.*

*One diesel engine tractor was key:
Deere's famous twin cylinder model G
A landmark tractor in my chronical
Easy to handle and so economical;
Exported worldwide, all rivals were cowered:
The story of tractors is a study of power.*

SCENE 5

LUDMILLA's GRAVE.

LUDMILLA is knitting. NADEZHDA and VERA enter and sit on either side of her.

VALENTINA enters rocking and cooing gently to a baby. DUBOV stands nect to her and the two gaze lovingly at the newborn.

VERA: I can't believe it's finally over. Have you seen the baby?

NADEZHDA: No. But it's a girl.

VERA: And her and Stanislav are going back with Dubov?

NADEZHDA: Yes.

VERA: Now we just have to persuade Pappa to go into sheltered housing.

NADEZHDA: Mike's working on that.

VERA: Pappa listens to Mike.

NADEZHDA: Because he's a man.

VERA: Sexist sod.

NADEZHDA: Yeah.

VERA: Who do you think is the father? Eric Pyke or Bald Ed? Or Bob Turner?

NADEZHDA: Or someone else?

VERA: Ha!

NADEZHDA: I think she really loves Dubov – the way she came rushing over as soon as she knew he was here.

VERA: And yet she abandoned him for Pappa.

NADEZHDA: The lure of life in the West. Imagine abandoning the love of your life for Pappa, and then finding out he isn't even rich. All he has to offer is a British passport – and that paid for by Bob Turner. I feel sorry for her – sometimes.

VERA: You are hopeless! She pities us Nadia. Thinks we're stupid, ugly and flat chested.

NADEZHDA: The thing I can't understand is what Dubov sees in her. He seems so...perspicacious. You'd think he could see through her.

VERA: It's her tits. All men are the same.

NADEZHDA laughs.

Except for your Mike. He's a good man.

NADEZHDA looks surprised at this compliment.

NADEZHDA: Pappa said something happened to you in the camp at Drachensee. Something about cigarettes. Can you remember?

VERA: Of course I can remember.

NADEZHDA: Please Vera. Tell me.

VERA: Why are you so desperate to know?

NADEZHDA: Because you're my big sister and something happened to you that you've buried.

VERA: It's not buried treasure. Much uglier than that.

NADEZHDA: Mum's dead. I can't ask her, though I wish I had.

Pappa – well Pappa is full of stories that make little sense. Only you can tell me the truth. It's my family history too Vera.

VERA looks at NADEZHDA slightly frightened. LUDMILLA looks at VERA with love and strokes her hair.

VERA: Alright.

As VERA starts to tell her story, the atmosphere changes. We hear the sounds of a concentration camp, marching, German officers shouting orders, gun shots, crying etc.

VERA: The labour camp at Drachensee was a huge, ugly, chaotic and cruel place. Forced labourers from Poland, Ukraine, Belarus, conscripted to boost the German war effort, communists and trade unionists sent from the Low Countries for re education. Gypsies, homosexuals, Jews in transit to their deaths, inmates of lunatic asylums and captured resistance fighters all lived crushed together in low concrete lice-infested barracks. And the rule of terror was reinforced at every level.

In the next section, all members of the cast /ENSEMBLE dramatise the camp as VERA tells the story of what happened to her. VERA herself transforms herself into a shy, mousy ten year old.

VERA: Among the children of the forced labourers, the head of the gang was a sixteen-year-old youth called Kishka.

KISHKA enters. He swaggers and smokes. He catches sight of VERA and pushes her around.

KISHKA: *(Calls out.)* Oy! You – mouse! You! What is your name?

VERA: Vera.

KISHKA: Vera! You know you have to pay a tax here.

VERA: Tax?

KISHKA: Cigarette tax.

VERA: I – don't – I don't smoke.

KISHKA: Not for you, you idiot. All kids here have to collect cigarettes for us.

VERA: How?

KISHKA: I don't care how. Get them from your parents.

VERA: But my parents don't smoke. And the cigarettes they get, they trade for food.

KISHKA: Then you'll just have to steal from someone else.

VERA: I can't steal.

KISHKA punches and kicks VERA and then grabs her by her collar, shaking her violently.

KISHKA: Are you thick or something? Everyone else pays their cigarette tax around here – except for you. I can't let you get away with that can I? Wouldn't be fair on the others.

KISHKA lets go of VERA who scampers off.

KISHKA: *(Calls back.)* Don't come back empty handed or you'll get a proper beating.

VERA is desperate. She scurries around searching everywhere. She sees a Nazi uniform jacket hanging on a peg. Quick as a flash, she pulls out a packet of cigarettes and slips them into a pocket and scarpers. She runs straight to KISHKA and hands over her packet of cigarettes.

KISHKA looks at the packet.

KISHKA: Hey, good work mouse. Army cigarettes! These are nice and strong. Not bad. Not bad at all mouse.

KISHKA ruffles VERA's hair and sits and smokes. VERA crouches nearby and watches him afraid.

The NAZI officer returns and takes his jacket off the nail. He puts the jacket on and buttons it up, placing his hand in his pocket as he searches for his cigarettes. He flies into a rage, shouting and cursing.

NAZI OFFICER: Where are my cigarettes? I had a whole packet in here! Fuckers! Has anyone seen the thief who stole them? Someone must know – if you don't own up, I'll punish the whole block. You fucking peasants! Do you hear me? You'll all go straight to the Correction block and hardly anyone comes out of there alive. D'you hear me? Kishka! Kishka!

The NAZI OFFICER drags KISHKA in and searches him roughly, finding the cigarettes.

NAZI OFFICER: I knew it would be you. Scum, thief, little fucking rat. Where are the rest? There was a whole packet!

The NAZI OFFICER officer continually slaps KISHKA making him cry.

KISHKA: Please sir, please…no… it wasn't me…please… ouch…arghhh…

NAZI OFFICER: I'll teach you not to steal from me you street rat.

KISHKA: Please sir. It was her – that skinny one over there – she nicked them and gave them all out to the kids.

> *KISHKA points at VERA. The NAZI OFFICER marches straight to VERA.*

NAZI OFFICER: You – was it?

> *The NAZI OFFICER grabs VERA by the collar and drags her, pushing and punching. VERA screams and cries.*

NAZI OFFICER: Get in there you little bitch.

> *The NAZI OFFICER throws VERA into a room and locks it. We can hear VERA screaming and crying from inside.*
>
> *KISHKA watches for a moment and then exits quickly. LUDMILLA enters.*

LUDMILLA: *(Calling.)* Vera! Vera?

VERA: *(From inside.)* Mamma! Mamma!

> *The NAZI OFFICER smirks.*

NAZI OFFICER: Your daughter is a thieving bitch. Stole all my cigarettes. She needs to be taught a lesson.

LUDMILLA: No, please. She didn't know what she was doing. The big ones put her up to it. What does she want with cigarettes? Can't you see what a stupid little thing she is?

NAZI OFFICER: Stupid, but I need a smoke. You'll have to give me yours.

LUDMILLA: I don't have any. Sorry. I traded them. I don't smoke. Next week, when we get paid – you can have them all.

NAZI OFFICER: What use is next week? I need a smoke now and your dirty thieving sniveling kid stole them all.

> *The NAZI OFFICER produces a cat whip and starts to flick LUDMILLA around the legs with it.*

LUDMILLA: Please, she's just a child.

NAZI OFFICER: You Ukrainians are ungrateful swine. We save you from the Communists. We bring you to our country, we feed you, we give you work. And all you can think of is to steal from us. Bastards.

LUDMILLA: Please, forgive us.

NAZI OFFICER: You have to be punished. We have a correction block for vermin like you. You know the F Block?

LUDMILLA: No! Have pity!

NAZI OFFICER: You must have heard how nicely we look after you there.

> *The NAZI OFFICER unlocks the door and drags VERA screaming out by the hair. LUDMILLA pulls VERA towards her.*

LUDMILLA: You seem such a nice young man. Please spare us. Forgive us young man. Show us mercy.

NAZI OFFICER: I'll show you mercy. We won't separate you from your child. You'll go in with her, vermin mother. You'll be at home, like rats in a sewer.

LUDMILLA: Why must you do this? Don't you have a mother? A sister?

NAZI OFFICER: Why are you talking about my mother? She is a good German woman.

> *The NAZI OFFICER grabs both VERA and LUDMILLA and exits, dragging them as they cry.*

SCENE 6

We see LUDMILLA and VERA are clinging to each other crying in a cage which is very narrow – like an upright coffin.

NIKOLAI is in another one, huddled at the bottom.

There is a small amount of light coming in from the top and they all reach up with their arms.

NAZI OFFICER: (OS) We'll teach you to raise your children not to steal. You will be re-educated. And your vermin husband. You will *all* be corrected.

> *There is the sound of the cage being slammed shut with an almighty crash of steel as the lights go out.*

SCENE 7

We go back to VERA and NADEZHDA beneath the cherry tree. NADEZHDA takes VERA's hand and they sit in silence for a beat. LUDMILLA is there too.

VERA: I'm a war time baby and you're a peace time baby. That's the difference between us.

NADEZHDA looks upset.

NADEZHDA: I'm sorry I got so possessive over Mum's locket. Of course she wanted you to have it.

SCENE 8

VALENTINA enters with her baby. NADIA enters and coos over the baby.

NADEZHDA: Oh, Valentina. She is beautiful.

VALENTINA: I think so. Name is Margaritka. Is name of my friend Margaritka Zadchuk.

NADEZHDA: Lovely.

VALENTINA: And is name of your most famous English president.

NADEZHDA: I'm sorry?

VALENTINA: Mrs Tatsher.

NADEZHDA: Ah.

(To the baby.) Baby Maggie. May all your wildest dreams come true. Have a good life.

NADEZHDA kisses the baby on the forehead. VALENTINA smiles.

DUBOV enters and takes the baby expertly off VALENTINA. She fetches a bottle which she hands over to DUBOV and then she exits. DUBOV sits and feeds the baby. NIKOLAI is rummaging around in his papers again.

NIKOLAI: Final installment.

NIKOLAI reads as NADEZHDA, MIKE and DUBOV all sit and listen/join in, reading it out in turns. The

ENSEMBLE joins in too. Perhaps this last Tractors poem can be done to Ukranian music.

POEM 5

NIKOLAI: *If given respect and appropriate space*
Technology can benefit the human race
But used without appropriate control
Technology can take a deadly toll.
Humility is the critical factor
As we learn from the history of the tractor.

The role of the tractor, I've already addressed,
In opening the prairies of America's west
But what happened next is a lesson for all
How humanity's greed can be our downfall.
In pursuit of profit, arrogant and proud,
Midwest farmers ploughed and ploughed.

Drought and strong winds blew away the earth
And the dustbowl was formed, a cruel birth;
Hardship ensued from nature's backlash,
Leading towards the Wall Street Crash;
And chaos and poverty offered baptism
To the rise of division and of facism.

Dear reader I hope that now you concede
That nature's nature is one we must heed;
There are forces with which we must not interfere
Use wisely the knowledge of your engineer.
Don't let technology be your master
Abusing its power will lead to disaster.

This is my message, the moral is plain
From the history of tractors in Ukraine

NIKOLAI stops and looks to his audience.

Everyone erupts into cheers.

MIKE: Well done! Excellent ending!

NADEZHDA: Bravo Pappa!

DUBOV: Bravo Nikolai Alexeevich!

NIKOLAI gets busy tying up the manuscript in brown paper and string.

NIKOLAI: Please, Volodya Simeonovich. Take it with you to Ukraina. Maybe someone will publish it there.

DUBOV: No, no! This is your life's work!

NIKOLAI: Pah!

DUBOV: I cannot take it.

NIKOLAI: It is finished now. Take it please. I have another book to write.

DUBOV stands up and takes the manuscript with his free hand. VALENTINA enters with STANISLAV in tow. He is carrying bags and baby things. Everybody exchanges hugs and kisses, apart from Nikolai and VALENTINA who manage to avoid each other. The DUBOV's exit as MIKE, NADEZHDA and NIKOLAI stand FOS and wave their goodbyes. We hear the roar of the Rolls Royce engine as it backs out of the drive.

NIKOLAI: Goodbye! Goodbye! Drive carefully.

They all carry on waving as we hear the engine of the car disappear into the distance. LUDMILLA quietly enters carrying her suitcase, now with her coat back on.

NADEZHDA: Do you feel sad Pappa?

NIKOLAI: First time when Valentina left was sad. This time, not so sad. She is beautiful woman, but maybe I did not make her happy. Dubov is good type. He will look after her.

NIKOLAI moves back into the lounge followed by MIKE and NADEZHDA.

NIKOLAI looks at his map on his lounge floor and walks over the map, pointing out landmarks.

NIKOLAI: Look here. Later they will cross from Felixstowe to Hamburg, next to Berlin. Cross into Poland at Guben.

Then Wroclav, Krakow, cross border at Przemysl. Ukraina. Home.

NIKOLAI falls silent staring at the map. LUDMILLA stands by him and stares at the map too.

MIKE: You okay old man?

LUDMILLA: This is our journey. Ukraina to England.

NIKOLAI traces the journey backwards.

NIKOLAI: Same journey, other direction. Fleeing the war.

NADEZHDA: What happened in the war Pappa?

NIKOLAI: People died.

LUDMILLA: Those who were brave perished first. Those who believed in something died for a belief. Those who survived...

NIKOLAI: You know more than twenty million Soviet citizens perished in the war.

MIKE: The number – it's so vast – so unknowable.

NIKOLAI: And there's Drachensee – near Kiel. I was there in that camp during war with Ludmilla and Vera.

NADEZHDA: Vera said something about a Correction block?

NIKOLAI: Aha, this was very unfortunate episode caused by cigarettes and Vera. She was just ten years old. Lucky the war ended then. British came just in time – rescued us from Correction block. Otherwise...

MIKE: How long were you in there for?

NIKOLAI waves away the question.

NIKOLAI: Lucky also that at liberation we were in British zone. Ludmilla's birthplace, Novaya Aleksandria

NADEZHDA: Why was that lucky?

NIKOLAI: Because that was formerly part of Poland and Poles were allowed to stay in West. Under Churchill-Stalin agreement, Poles could stay in England, Ukrainians sent back. Most sent to Siberia – most perished. Lucky Millochka still had birth certificate. Lucky I had some work papers. Said I come from Dashev. Germans wrote it down differently, changed Cyrillic to Roman script. Dashev Daszewo. Word sounds the same but Dashev is in Ukraina, Daszewo is in Poland and. Ha ha. Lucky immigration officer believed. So much luck in such a short time – enough to last a lifetime.

MIKE: Wow Nikolai. Can't believe I never knew all this. It's mind blowing.

NADEZHDA: What happened in the Correction Block?

NIKOLAI: It's in the past now. The main thing is that to survive is to win.

LUDMILLA takes a last look at NIKOLAI and NADEZHDA, picks up her suitcase, puts on her hat and coat and exits.

SCENE 9

NADEZHDA, VERA and NIKOLAI wait in an office. NADEZHDA is fussing over NIKOLAI's hair, trying to smooth it down.

NADEZHDA: Remember Pappa, this is important. You must be polite and look like you want to come here.

NIKOLAI: Yes, yes. I am not baby. You don't need to tell me how to behave! But they have to behave too – if they are like a nurse Stalin, I am not coming here.

VERA: Pappa! You must try and fit in with the other residents. Do you understand?

NADEZHDA: Yes, in your own flat you can do what you like, but when you're with the others, you must try and behave in a normal way. You don't want them to think you're crazy do you?

NIKOLAI: *Tak tak.*

> *BEVERLEY enters. She is smiley, middle aged and blonde. (Not at all dissimilar to VALENTINA.)*

BEVERLEY: Ah! Mr Mayevskyj – I am pronouncing right aren't I?

NIKOLAI: Yes.

BEVERLEY: I am delighted to meet you at last.

> *NIKOLAI is smitten. He stands and takes BEVERLEY's hand.*

NIKOLAI: The pleasure is all mine.

> *NIKOLAI bows and kisses BEVERLEY's hand. BEVERLEY laughs.*

BEVERLEY: Oh! So gallant! I can see we're going to get on well. Please do sit down. I've met your lovely daughters before. Hello again. I am the warden here and my name's Beverley. You can call me Bev.

NIKOLAI: And you can call me Nikolai.

BEVERLEY: Such a lovely name. Now I wanted to meet you in person, just to make sure you know all about us.

NIKOLAI: I have studied the brochures.

BEVERLEY: Excellent. I've seen all your Doctor's letters and notes and I do think this is just the place for you. We have a waiting list, but I've bumped you up, because I think you would fit in well here. As long as you're happy today, I think there's a room becoming available next week.

> *BEVERLEY adjusts her top a bit. NIKOLAI smiles.*

BEVERLEY: Nikolai, here at Sunny bank sheltered housing complex, we have forty-six flats and lovely residents – a communal lounge where residents can watch television…

> *NIKOLAI grimaces.*

NIKOLAI: I only watch the news.

BEVERLEY: We also have coffee mornings.

NIKOLAI: I prefer apple juice.

BEVERLEY: We can do apple juice for you. Nice gardens with rose beds and chairs for you to sit out in the sun. We even have a resident owl! You could take part in our ballroom dancing lessons…

NIKOLAI: I like gardens. But my wife, she was the gardener. And oh – how my Millochka could dance!

BEVERLEY: It's hard isn't it, when our loved ones pass on. I lost my husband three years ago. Miss him like crazy. Maybe you and I could do a little ballroom dancing and remember the old times together – eh?

NIKOLAI: I would be honoured.

BEVERLEY: There are chess championships and quiz nights and oh – yoga classes.

NIKOLAI: Aha!

NADEZHDA: And my husband and I are nearby so we can visit regularly, go out for trips.

BEVERLEY: Sounds perfect. You'll be independent – do your own cooking and we can arrange for someone to do your shopping for you, if you like.

NIKOLAI: I will cook you my *piece de resistance* – Toshiba apples.

BEVERLEY: A Ukrainian dish? Excellent. I see you have a touch of arthritis, so we'll register you with the local doctor. His surgery's literally across the road, so it's very convenient. I was going to give you a quick tour if you'd like?

NIKOLAI: I will go here. Nowhere else.

BEVERLEY: Wonderful! I look forward to getting to know you. Come, let's take a turn around the place. I can show you a flat which'll be similar to yours. Nadezhda, you can come with us too if you like?

> *NIKOLAI stands and takes BEVERLEY's arm as she leads him out. VERA and NADEZHDA smile at each other and link arms. NIKOLAI turns, grins, winks and does a thumbs up sign at them as they all exit.*

END

BY THE SAME AUTHOR

Lions and Tigers
9781786821843

Anita and Me
9781783199310

Love N Stuff
9781783190553

Wah! Wah! Girls: A British Bollywood Musical
9781849431873

Fragile Land
9781840023671

Inside Out
9781840023527

Meet the Mukherjees
9781840028614

Sugar Mummies
9781840026559

Gladiator Games
9781840026245

Mind Walking
9781849435062

The Empress
9781849434904

White Boy
9781840028607

Sanctuary
9781840023022

Adaptations

The Country Wife
Based on William Wycherley
9781840025163

Great Expectations
Based on Charles Dickens
9781849431224

Hobson's Choice
Based on Harold Brighouse
9781840023831

Collections

Tanika Gupta: Political Plays
9781849432474

WWW.OBERONBOOKS.COM

Follow us on www.twitter.com/@oberonbooks
& www.facebook.com/OberonBooksLondon